MW01230388

# Studies in Perception and Action X

FIFTEENTH INTERNATIONAL CONFERENCE ON PERCEPTION AND ACTION

July 12–17, 2009
Minneapolis, Minnesota

EDITED BY
**Jeffrey B. Wagman** and **Christopher C. Pagano**

Routledge
Taylor & Francis Group

LONDON AND NEW YORK

Cover design by Rally Pagulayan

First published 2014 by Psychology Press

2 Park Square, Milton Park, Abingdon, Oxon OX14 4RN
711 Third Avenue, New York, NY 10017, USA

*Routledge is an imprint of the Taylor & Francis Group, an informa business*

First issued in hardback 2017

ISBN 978-1-84872-880-6 (pbk)
ISBN 978-1-138-45690-7 (hbk)

**Library of Congress Cataloging-in-Publication Data**

International Conference on Perception and Action (15th : 2009 : Minneapolis, Minn.)
  Studies in perception and action X : fifteenth International Conference on Perception and Action / [edited by] Jeffrey B. Wagman, Christopher C. Pagano.
    p. cm.
  "Contains research presented at the ICPA XV conference held in Minneapolis, Minnesota from July 12-17, 2009"--Preface.
  Includes bibliographical references.
  ISBN 978-1-84872-880-6 (pbk. : alk. paper)
  1. Perceptual-motor processes--Congresses. I. Wagman, Jeffrey B. II. Pagano, Christopher C. III. Title. IV. Title: Studies in perception and action 10.

BF295.I58 2010
153.7--dc22                                                              2009021262

**Visit the Taylor & Francis Web site at**
**http://www.taylorandfrancis.com**

**and the Psychology Press Web site at**
**http://www.psypress.com**

# Table of Contents

## Chapter 2: Interpersonal Coordination

## Chapter 3: Perception & Perceptual Learning

## Chapter 4: Perception of Affordances

**Chapter 5: Posture**

# Preface

The edited book series *Studies in Perception and Action* contains a collection of research presented as posters at the International Conference on Perception and Action (ICPA). The *Studies* series has appeared in conjunction with the biennial ICPA since 1991 when the conference was held in Amsterdam. The ICPA conference series provides a forum for presenting new data, theory, and methodology relevant to the ecological approach to perception-action. The *Studies* series is unique in that it provides a peer-reviewed mechanism for documenting these developments through brief articles that contain more detail than typical conference proceedings abstracts (e.g., method and results sections) but less detail than full-length book chapters or journal articles. As a result, the *Studies* series makes the ICPA conference proceedings available to a wide audience in a complete yet compact format. In many instances, the contributions to *Studies* represent the first appearance of new ideas in a scientific venue. As a result, the *Studies* volumes contain the most recent and cutting-edge research in perception and action.

This volume is the 10th in the *Studies in Perception and Action* series, and it contains research presented at the ICPA XV conference held in Minneapolis, Minnesota from July 12-17, 2009. The conference organizing committee co-chairs for ICPA XV were Tom Stoffregen and Mike Wade, both of the University of Minnesota. The 40 papers presented in this volume, reviewed by a scientific committee composed of distinguished perception-action researchers from six countries across four continents, represent the latest developments in ecological psychology research from laboratories around the world.

A significant challenge we faced in assembling this collection was organizing these diverse papers into coherent topic headings. Although many of the papers cut across topics (as is often the case with research in perception-action), we have done our best to organize the papers in a way that provides an initial structure for the reader. We have provided a list of keywords to assist the reader identifying papers on particular topics.

We thank William Mace of the International Society for Ecological Psychology (ISEP) for his support, and we thank Rally Pagulayan for the cover design. We are indebted to previous editors Sarah Cummins-Sebree, Michael A. Riley, and Kevin Shockley for their guidance and advice.

Jeffrey B. Wagman
Department of Psychology, Illinois State University

Christopher C. Pagano
Department of Psychology, Clemson University

# Meeting History

1.  1981 – Storrs, CT, USA
2.  1983 – Nashville, TN, USA
3.  1985 – Uppsala, SWEDEN
4.  1987 – Trieste, ITALY
5.  1989 – Miami, OH, USA
6.  1991 – Amsterdam, THE NETHERLANDS
7.  1993 – Vancouver, CANADA
8.  1995 – Marseilles, FRANCE
9.  1997 – Toronto, CANADA
10. 1999 – Edinburgh, SCOTLAND
11. 2001 – Storrs, CT, USA
12. 2003 – Gold Coast, QLD, AUSTRALIA
13. 2005 – Monterey, CA, USA
14. 2007 – Yokohama City, JAPAN
15. 2009 – Minneapolis, MN, USA

# Contributors

**Harrison Allen**, Department of Psychology, Brigham Young University

**Joshua Aman**, Human Sensorimotor Control Lab, School of Kinesiology, University of Minnesota, aman0038@umn.edu

**Dilip N. Athreya**, Department of Psychology, University of Cincinnati, athreyadilip@yahoo.com

**Laura Bachus**, University of Cincinnati, BachusLE@email.uc.edu

**Benoît G. Bardy**, Motor Efficiency and Deficiency Laboratory, University Montpellier 1, benoit.bardy@univ-montp1.fr

**Tom Beckstead**, Department of Psychology, Brigham Young University

**Geoffrey Bingham**, Department of Psychological and Brain Sciences, Indiana University, gbingham@indiana.edu

**Julia J. C. Blau**, Department of Psychology, University of Connecticut, Julia.Carroll@uconn.edu

**V. Bonnet**, University Montpellier II, France, bonnet@lirmm.com

**Danny Boysen**, Department of Psychology, Brigham Young University

**Blandine Bril**, École des Hautes Études en Sciences Sociales - Groupe de recherché "Apprentissage et Contexte," Paris, France, blandine.bril@ehess.fr

**Kimberly Capehart**, Department of Psychology, University of Cincinnati

**Wilson Cardwell**, Department of Psychology, Center for Ergonomic Research, Miami University, cardwewb@muohio.edu

**Claudia Carello**, Center for the Ecological Study of Perception and Action, University of Connecticut, claudia.carello@uconn.edu

**Fu-Chen Chen**, University of Minnesota, chen1619@umn.edu

**Tehran J. Davis,** Department of Psychology, University of Cincinnati, davtj@email.uc.edu

**Dobromir G. Dotov**, Department of Psychology, University of Connecticut, dobromir.dotov@uconn.edu

**Justin Fine**, Department of Psychology, University of Cincinnati

**Ross Flom,** Department of Psychology, Brigham Young University

**P. Fraisse**, University Montpellier II, France, fraisse@lirmm.fr

**Till D. Frank**, Center for the Ecological Study of Perception and Action, University of Connecticut, Till.Frank@uconn.edu

**Nobuhiro Furuyama**, National Institute of Informatics, furuyama@nii.ac.jp

**M. Russell Giveans**, University of Minnesota, givea017@umn.edu

**Akitoshi Hanazawa**, Kyushu Institute of Technology, Japan

**Shogo Hirata**, Tokyo Gakugei University, sghirata@hotmail.co.jp

**Naoya Hirose**, Kyoto Notre Dame University, nhirose@notredame.ac.jp

**Kathryn Hobbs**, Psychology Department, Smith College, khobbs@email.smith.edu

**Chia-Chun Huang**, Department of Physical Education, National Taiwan Normal University, Taipei, Taiwan.

**Yoshifumi Ikeda**, Department of Education for Children with Intellectual Disability, Tokyo Gakugei University, Japan, s081003p@u-gakugei.ac.jp

**Makoto Inagami**, Department of Built Environment, Tokyo Institute of Technology, Japan, inagami.m.aa@m.titech.ac.jp

**Hiroshi Inou**, DENSO Corporation, hiroshi_inou@denso.co.jp

**Robert W. Isenhower**, Center for the Ecological Study of Perception and Action, University of Connecticut, robert.isenhower@uconn.edu

**Kiyohide Ito**, Future University-Hakodate, itokiyo@fun.ac.jp

**Jacob Jones**, Department of Psychology, Brigham Young University

**Azizah J. Jor'dan**, University of Minnesota, jord0154@umn.edu

**Yu Kamiyama**, Department of Education for Children with Intellectual Disability, Tokyo Gakugei University, Japan, c053113p@u-gakugei.ac.jp

**So Kanazawa**, Japan Women's University, Japan

**Stephanie Karges**, Department of Psychology, Miami University, Oxford, Ohio

**Yasunobu Katsumata**, Toyohashi University of Technology, Japan

**Nam-Gyoon Kim**, Department of Psychology, Keimyung University, nk70@kmu.ac.kr

**Michiteru Kitazaki**, Toyohashi University of Technology, Japan

**Mitsuru Kokubun**, Tokyo Gakugei University, kokubun@u-gakugei.ac.jp

**Jüergen Konczak**, Human Sensorimotor Control lab, School of Kinesiology, University of Minnesota, jkonczak@umn.edu

**Masayuki Kumai**, Tohoku University, Japan

**Nikita A. Kuznetsov**, University of Cincinnati, nikitakuznetsov@yahoo.com

**Julien Lagarde,** Motor Efficiency and Deficiency Laboratory, University Montpellier, France, julien.lagarde@univ-montp1.fr

**Eric Littman**, Miami University, Oxford OH, Littmaem@muohio.edu

**Stacy M. Lopresti-Goodman,** Center for the Ecological Study of Perception and Action, University of Connecticut, stacy.lopresti-goodman@uconn.edu

**Chia-Hao Lu**, Human Sensorimotor control lab, School of Kinesiology, University of Minnesota, luxxx214@umn:edu

**Ludovic Marin,** Motor Efficiency and Deficiency Laboratory, University Montpellier 1, ludovic.marin@univ-montp1.fr

**Leonard S. Mark**, Department of Psychology, Center for Ergonomic Research, Miami University, markls@muohio.edu

**Kerry L. Marsh,** Center for the Ecological Study of Perception and Action, University of Connecticut, kerry.l.marsh@uconn.edu

**Shin Maruyama**, Research Organization of Information and Systems, National Institute of Informatics, Japan, shindiana2@yahoo.co.jp

**Dawn M. McBride**, Department of Psychology, Illinois State University

**Hiroyuki Mishima**, University of Fukui, Japan, hiromish@yb3.so-net.ne.jp

**Ryo Mizuno**, Graduate School of Systems Information Science Future University-Hakodate, Japan, g3107005@fun.ac.jp

**Tetsushi Nonaka**, University of Tokyo, nonaka.tetsushi@iii.u-tokyo.ac.jp

**Ryuzo Ohno**, Department of Built Environment, Tokyo Institute of Technology, Japan

**Makoto Okamoto**, School of System Information Science, Future University-Hakodate, Japan

**Hideyuki Okuzumi**, Tokyo Gakugei University, okuzumi@u-gakugei.ac.jp

**Edward W. Otten**, Miami University, Oxford OH, ottenew@muohio.edu

**Zsolt Palatinus**, Center for the Ecological Study of Perception and Action, University of Connecticut, zsolt.palatinus@uconn.edu

**Christie Pelzer**, University of Minnesota

**Milena Petrovic**, Department of Psychology, Center for Ergonomic Research, Miami University, petrovm@muohio.edu

**Amanda Phillippi**, Department of Psychology, Brigham Young University

**Peter B. Pufall**, Psychology Department, Smith College, ppufall@smith.edu

**N. Ramdani**, University Montpellier II, France, ramdani@lirmm.fr

**S. Ramdani**, University Montpellier I, France, sofiane.ramdani@univ-montp1.fr

**Veronica C. Ramenzoni**, Department of Psychology, University of Cincinnati, ramenzvc@email.uc.edu

**Robert Rein**, École des Hautes Études en Sciences Sociales - Groupe de Recherche Apprentissage et Contexte, Paris, France, mail@robertrein.de

**Michael J. Richardson**, Department of Psychology, Colby College, mjrichar@colby.edu

**Michael A. Riley**, Department of Psychology, University of Cincinnati, rileym@email.uc.edu

**Mamoru Sawada**, Corporate R&D Department, DENSO Corporation, Japan, mamoru_sawada@denso.co.jp

**R. C. Schmidt,** Department of Psychology, College of the Holy Cross, rschmidt@holycross.edu.

**Keonho Shin**, Department of Education, Kangnam University, Yongin, Korea

**Kevin Shockley**, Department of Psychology, University of Cincinnati, kevin.shockley@uc.edu

**Jonathan Shook**, Department of Psychology, University of Cincinnati

**Paula Silva,** Center for the Ecological Study of Perception and Action, University of Connecticut, paula.silva@uconn.edu

**L. James Smart, Jr.**, Department of Psychology. Miami University, Oxford, OH, Smartlj@muohio.edu

**Alison Smith**, University of Minnesota

**Damian G. Stephen**, Center for the Ecological Study of Perception and Action, University of Connecticut, damian.stephen@uconn.edu

**Thomas A. Stoffregen**, University of Minnesota, tas@umn.edu

**Adam Strang**, Department of Psychology, Miami University, Oxford, Ohio

**Masashi Takiyama,** University of Tokyo, masaphy@iainukiki.jp.

**Aki Tsuruhara**, Department of Psychology, Chuo University, Tokyo, Japan, aki.tsuruhara@gmail.com

**Michael T. Turvey**, Center for the Ecological Study of Perception and Action, University of Connecticut, michael.turvey@uconn.edu

**Masaki Ueno**, Department of Education for Children with Intellectual Disability, Tokyo Gakugei University, Japan, c053109p@u-gakugei.ac.jp

**Manuel Varlet**, Efficiency and Deficiency Laboratory, University Montpellier1, Montpellier, France

**Sebastien Villard,** University of Minnesota, svillard@umn.edu

**Michael G. Wade,** University of Minnesota, mwade@umn.edu

**Jeffrey B. Wagman,** Department of Psychology, Illinois State University, jbwagma@ilstu.edu

**Eliah J. White**, Department of Psychology, University of Cincinnati, whiteej@email.uc.edu

**Melissa Wright**, Department of Psychology, Brigham Young University

**Masami Yamaguchi**, Chuo University, Japan

**Chih-Mei (Melvin) Yang**, Department of Physical Education, National Taiwan Normal University, Taipei, Taiwan, melvin@ntnu.edu.tw

**Lin Ye**, Department of Psychology, Center for Ergonomic Research, Miami University, yel@muohio.edu

**Ken Yoshida**, University of Minnesota, yoshi028@umn.edu

**Yawen Yu**, University of Minnesota

**Qin (Arthur) Zhu**, Motor Learning/Control Program, Division of Kinesiology and Health, University of Wyoming, qzhu1@uwyo.edu

# Chapter 1:

# Action & Coordination

*Studies in Perception & Action X*
J. B. Wagman & C. C. Pagano (Eds.)
© 2009 Taylor & Francis Group, LLC

# Nonlinear Attractor Dynamics and Symmetry Breaking in Prism Adaptation and Re-adaptation

Julia J. C. Blau[1], Damian G. Stephen[1], Till D. Frank[1],
M.T. Turvey[1,2], & Claudia Carello[1]

[1]Center for the Ecological Study of Perception and Action, University of Connecticut, USA, [2]Haskins Laboratories, New Haven, CT USA.

The typical prism adaptation paradigm consists of three phases (Fig. 1, panel 1). In the *baseline* phase, participants throw to a target to establish their average natural deviation from the target. During *adaptation*, participants wear prism goggles that shift their gaze. The disturbed vision results in an initial systematic deviation from the target, and exponential error decay as the participant adapts to the perturbed perception-action system. The prism goggles are removed for the third phase, *re-adaptation*. At this point, the perception-action system is still adapted to the perturbation, which results in systematic error in the opposite direction of the original error, known as the aftereffect. This aftereffect is eliminated exponentially over the rest of the phase.

**Prism Adaptation—An Extended Case.** An extension of the paradigm reveals that when experimental conditions (presence of a wrist weight; Fernandez-Ruiz et al., 2000) differ during adaptation and re-adaptation phases (symmetry breaking), then re-adaptation is only partial. Performance error (aftereffect) does decay; however, when experimental conditions are re-established (symmetry regained), performance error returns (latent aftereffect) and another re-adaptation process occurs.

**Error Decay and the Dynamic Systems Approach.** Adaptation, the error decay of the aftereffect, and the latent aftereffect all exhibit gradual, exponential error decay, rather than one-trial learning. One explanation of this phenomenon is that the system is only calibrated for fine-tuning, with a maximum step per throw (Fernandez-Ruiz & Diaz, 2006). However, a dynamical systems approach might offer new insights. Dynamic systems theory is a powerful approach to examining perception-action systems (Beek et al., 1995; Kelso, 1995). Learning approached from this perspective has been associated with the emergence of attractors and self-organized states (Schöner & Kelso, 1995). We propose a dynamic model for prism adaptation.

**The Model.** Evolution of distance-to-target, $x(t)$, depends on the intrinsic attractor, $V_O$, and the adaptation attractor, $V_A$. The intrinsic attractor is invariant; the adaptation attractor emerges during an adaptation process and vanishes in the course of a re-adaptation process. The evolution of $x(t)$ is defined by:

$$\frac{d}{dt}x(t) = -\frac{d}{dx}V_0(x) - \frac{\partial}{\partial x}V_A(x,t) = -\frac{\partial}{\partial x}V(x,t)$$

where $V(x,t)$ is the total potential $V_O(x) + V_A(x,t)$. $V_O$ and $V_A$ can be modelled explicitly and predictions can be derived (Fig. 1, first two columns) by solving the model equation numerically and analytically (Frank, Blau, & Turvey, 2009). For an adaptation process we studied a model equation of the form:

$$\frac{d}{dt}x(t) = -b(x-s) - c\alpha(t)(x-s-\alpha(t))$$

$$\frac{d}{dt}\alpha(t) = I(x(t))$$

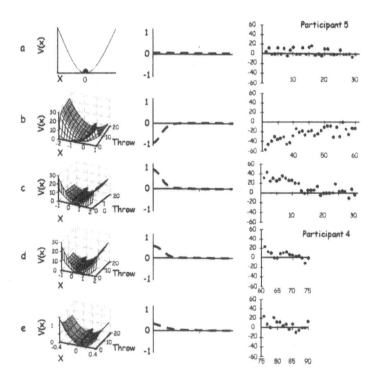

*Figure 1.* Explicit models (first column), predictions (second column) and examples of corresponding results (third column) in the general (panels a-c) and extended (panels d and e) prism adaptation paradigm.

where $s$ is the prismatic shift, and $\alpha$ is a time-dependent function of the adaptation potential $V_A$ (Fig. 1a, b). For the re-adaptation dynamics, $s = 0$ (Fig. 1c). For the extended prism paradigm, we add a constant term, $\delta$, that accounts for the symmetry-breaking (Fig. 1d). For the secondary adaptation process $\delta = 0$ (Fig. 1e). (See Frank, Blau, & Turvey, 2009, for a full explication of the model).

In this model, the symmetry-breaking term, $\delta$, must be defined experimentally. Although mass has been suggested as a possibility, the mass manipulation of Fernandez-Ruiz et al. (2000) is conflated with rotational inertia. These variables are disentangled in our experiment by placing a given mass at one of two locations on the arm, thereby manipulating rotational inertia while keeping mass constant. This also offers us the opportunity to compare our model predictions to actual experimental data (Fig. 1).

### Method

Forty undergraduates with normal or corrected-to-normal vision were assigned randomly to one of five groups defined by when, where, or whether prisms and weights were added or removed (Fig. 2). On each trial, a 108 g beanbag was thrown to a target 2.5 m away. Prisms (30-diopter Fresnel lenses) shifted vision to the left. A 1.15 kg band attached at the elbow brought about a smaller change in rotational inertia than that same band attached at the wrist.

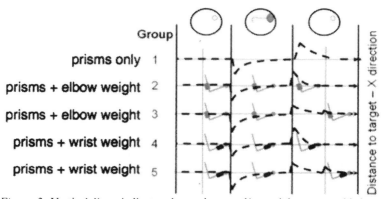

*Figure 2.* Vertical lines indicate when prisms and/or weights were added or removed. Results are symbolized by the dashed line. By convention, deviations below the horizontal line are to the left.

### Results and Discussion

**Model Fit.** In all cases, the data fit the model predictions (Fig. 1, last column), suggesting that a dynamical systems model can account for gradual learning behaviour such as prism adaptation. The model was also able to account for the symmetry breaking (Fig. 1d, e).

**Symmetry Breaking Term.** The first aftereffect was smaller and the latent aftereffect was greater in groups 3 and 5 than in groups 2 and 4, $F(1, 30) =$

12.82, $p < .002$, confirming the existence of the latent aftereffect under conditions of symmetry breaking (Fig. 2). In Groups 1, 3, and 5, the first aftereffect declined and the latent aftereffect increased across groups, $F(2, 21) = 13.94$, $p < .0001$, suggesting that rotational inertia, not mass, is the variable responsible for the symmetry breaking. Further research should uncover more variables that cause such a break in an effort to discover the underlying cause (see Blau, Stephen, Carello, & Turvey, under review, for a full discussion).

**General Discussion.** Prism adaptation does not exhibit one-trial learning. Prism adaptation is a dynamic process that can be described in terms of an evolution equation. Adaptation processes involve the emergence of behavioural patterns. Our modelling approach reveals that these patterns emerge in a nonlinear system. In short, our analysis suggests that adaptation requires nonlinearities. The context-dependency of prism adaptation can be understood as breaking the symmetry of conditions during adaptation and re-adaptation. Taking a dynamic systems perspective, symmetry-breaking reveals itself as an additive force. By fitting the proposed model to experimental data, meaningful parameters can be derived. Since the study of prism adaptation has clinical relevance (Brooks et al., 2007), these parameters could be used for diagnostic purposes.

**References**

Beek, P. J., Peper, C. E., & Stegeman, D. F. (1995). Dynamical models of movement coordination. *Human Movement Sciences, 14,* 573-608.

Blau, J. J. C., Stephen, D. G., Carello, C., & Turvey, M. T. (under review). Prism adaptation of underhand throwing: Rotational inertia and the primary and latent aftereffects.

Brooks, R. L., Nicholson, R. I., & Fawcett, A. J. (2007). Prisms throw light on developmental disorders. *Neurophysiologica, 45,* 1921-1930.

Fernández-Ruiz, J., & Díaz, R. (2006). Prism adaptation and aftereffect: Specifying the properties of a procedural memory system. *Learning & Memory, 7,* 193-198.

Fernández-Ruiz, J., Hall-Haro, C., Díaz, R., Mischner, J., Vergara, P., & Lopez-Garcia, J. C. (2000) Learning motor synergies makes use of information on muscular load. *Learning & Memory, 7,* 193-198.

Frank, T. D., Blau, J. J. C., & Turvey, M. T. (2009). Ninlinear attractor dynamics in the fundamental and extended prism adaptation paradigm. *Physics Letters A, 373(11),* 1022-1030.

Kelso, J. A. S. (1995) *Dynamic patterns.* MIT Press: Cambridge, MA.

Schöner, G. S. & Kelso, J. A. S. (1988). A synergetic theory of environmentally-specified and learned patterns of movement coordination: I. Relative phase dynamics. *Biological Cybernetics, 58,* 71-80.

*Acknowledgments.* This research was supported by National Science Foundation grant SBR 04-23036.

*Studies in Perception & Action X*
J. B. Wagman & C. C. Pagano (Eds.)
© 2009 Taylor & Francis Group, LLC

# Functional Tuning of Action to Task Constraints in Tool-Use: The Case of Stone Knapping

Blandine Bril, Robert Rein, & Tetsushi Nonaka

École des Hautes Études en Sciences Sociales, France

Tool use appears as a privileged entry to understand goal directed actions, the organism being not simply directed *toward* the goal, but rather directed *by* the goal (Shaw, 1987). The aim of the current study is to characterize the expertise in the earliest known instance of human tool-use, *stone knapping*, from the perspective where the emphasis is on the goal while the movement is viewed as driven by task constraints.

In stone knapping, one stone (*hammer*) is used to strike another (*core*) to remove a sharp-edged piece (*flake*) according to the fracture mechanism called conchoidal fracture. Counter intuitively, in conchoidal fracture, it has been demonstrated that the force of the blow does not play a major role in determining the dimension of the detached flake (Dibble & Pelcin, 1995). It does, however, play a critical role in determining whether or not a flake can be produced in the first place. Therefore, kinetic energy of the hammer at impact is one of the essential task constraints for flake production, and we hypothesized that if actions are controlled in a functionally specific manner, knappers would maintain the kinetic energy of the hammer at impact invariant irrespective of the mass of hammers used. In other words, the achievement of the goal, the removal of a flake, is driven in such a way to meet the constraints of the task, that is, to produce the required kinetic energy of the hammer at impact of the strike.

## Method

Nine participants with different knapping experience (two experts, three intermediates and four novices) participated in the experiment. Two hammers with different mass (heavy: 400g, light: 250g) were used. Flint weighing between 2-3 kg was used as cores. Striking movements were recorded using an Ascension miniBIRD© magnetic marker system set at a recording frequency of 100Hz. One sensor was attached to the backside of the hand. Each participant produced twenty flakes with each hammer. The trajectory length of the hammer was calculated based on the trajectory of the hand sensor in 3D space from the maximum vertical height to the point of impact. The kinetic energy was calculated using the formula $E_{kin} = \frac{1}{2} m \, v^2$ (v = resultant velocity). A linear mixed-model analysis incorporating hammer weight and skill level in the fixed-effects structure and subject as a random effect was used for statistical analysis, and Bonferroni-corrected post-hoc tests were used for multiple comparisons.

### Results and Discussion

590 strikes contributed to the analysis. Success rate of flaking per group was 84% for experts, 55% for intermediates, and 49% for novices.

*Hammer trajectory length.* Statistical analysis indicated a significant main effect for hammer weight, $F(1, 577) = 79.1$, $p<.001$, as well as a significant interaction between hammer weight and skill level, $F(1, 577) = 3.8$, $p < .05$. Participants used longer trajectories when striking with the lighter hammer.

*Velocity at impact.* Statistical analysis for striking velocity indicated a significant main effect for hammer weight, $F(1, 577) = 52.4$, $p < .001$.

*Kinetic energy.* Statistical analysis indicated significant differences between hammer conditions, $F(1, 577) = 14.3$, $p < .001$. Post-hoc test further revealed that there were no significant differences in kinetic energy between hammer conditions for experts, while the differences for intermediates and novices were both significant ($p < .01$). All remaining effects were nonsignificant.

The results of the experiment showed that modern stone knappers adjust their movements according to task constraints. When using a lighter hammer participants across all groups increased the velocity of the hammer to achieve perceived necessary kinetic energies. However, only expert knappers were able to adjust their movement kinematics in a way which left the resulting kinetic energy unaltered between hammer conditions. In contrast, novice and intermediate skilled knappers exhibited different kinetic energies between the two conditions due to disproportional increases in striking velocity for the lighter hammer. The results indicate that knapping skill is characterized by functional tuning to task constraints. In addition, a general trend was observed where the strikes of experts tend to involve lower kinetic energy compared to novice and intermediate knappers. The fact that the success rate of detachment of flakes by strikes was highest for experts and lowest for novices implies that kinetic energy for novices was more than what was needed to detach a flake, while experts controlled their actions just sufficient to achieve the goal. The results stress the influence of perceptual parameters for the control of actions. For successful action, the actor must establish the functional relationship between himself, the tool, and the environment.

Overall, the results of this study highlight the importance of detecting the constraints of the task, and regulating actions accordingly. The characteristics of expert skills we found, fits nicely to the definition of dexterity given by Bernstein, who wrote "Dexterity is the ability to create a perfect key for any emerging lock (Bernstein, 1996, p. 215).

*Table 1.* Means and standard deviations of dependent variables over all strikes

| Skill Level | Hammer | Trajectory Length(cm) | | Velocity (m/s) | | Kinetic Energy(J) | |
|---|---|---|---|---|---|---|---|
| | | M | SD | M | SD | M | SD |
| Expert | Light | 21.91 | 6.81 | 3.39 | 0.55 | 5.91 | 2.01 |
| | Heavy | 14.13 | 2.83 | 2.75 | 0.72 | 4.37 | 2.42 |
| Intermediate | Light | 28.40 | 9.20 | 4.93 | 1.48 | 12.47 | 7.75 |
| | Heavy | 27.32 | 10.87 | 4.28 | 1.51 | 11.42 | 8.04 |
| Novice | Light | 26.67 | 5.10 | 4.10 | 1.85 | 9.45 | 10.61 |
| | Heavy | 21.90 | 3.75 | 3.03 | 1.00 | 5.28 | 5.27 |

**References**

Bernstein, N. A. (1996). *Dexterity and Its Development*. Mahwah, NJ: Lawrence Erlbaum Associates.

Dibble, H. L., & Pelcin, A. (1995). The Effect of Hammer Mass and Velocity on Flake Mass. *J. Archaeol. Sci, 22*, 429-439.

Shaw, R. E. (1987). Behavior with a purpose [Review of the book *Goal-Directed Behavior*]. *Contemporary Psychology, 32*, 243-245.

*Acknowledgements.* This research was funded by the European Union project HANDTOMOUTH.

*Studies in Perception & Action X*
J. B. Wagman & C. C. Pagano (Eds.)
© 2009 Taylor & Francis Group, LLC

# Variability of Uni-Manual Pendulum Oscillation at and away from Resonance

Dobromir G. Dotov[1], Damian G. Stephen[1], Till D. Frank[1], & M. T. Turvey[1,2]

[1]Center for the Ecological Study of Perception and Action, University of Connecticut
[2]Haskins Laboratories

Extensive research based on the dual-pendulum paradigm (Kugler & Turvey, 1987) has helped to establish overarching dynamical laws of intra- and inter-personal coordination (Amazeen, Amazeen, & Turvey, 1998). Can the study of uni-manual pendulum oscillation too be informative about dynamic constraints on motor behavior and coordination? In order to address this question our experiment focused on the coordination between the rhythmic motor behavior of swinging a hand-held pendulum and an auditory metronome as an environmental stimulus. Previous research with the same design (using phase space reconstruction to characterize the dynamics) found that the system could be described as having fewer active degrees of freedom, less noise, and a greater prediction horizon when running at its resonance as compared to when running at lower or higher rates (Goodman, Riley, Mitra, & Turvey, 2000). In this way, the "comfort" that the central nervous system experienced in a resonant configuration could be defined in terms of minimization of controlled variables and maximization of predictability of chaotic dynamics.

In order to extend the understanding of such a system, we delved further into the issue of variability. A vast array of research provides evidence that variability of motor behavior is not just noise extrinsic to the movement determinism but actually plays an essential role in helping the system establish its functionally appropriate behavior (for a review see, Riley & Turvey, 2002). In this respect, Abarbanel suggests that "the range of alternatives available to which one can control a system is larger if chaotic motion, seen as a wide ranging exploration of state space, is allowed" (1996, p. vi). We can sharpen our initial question by using Abarbanel's insight as a guiding intuition. What can the properties of the oscillation variability tell us about the system? Does pushing it away from resonance mean pushing it away from its stable state, thus, inducing a potential for the system to search for alternative stable states? Is the amount and structure of variability going to express this potential?

To begin answering these questions, we used drift-diffusion analysis based on generalized Langevin equation seeking to reconstruct the stochastic dynamics of frequency entrainment. This approach has been recommended in light of its potential ability to emphasize the intrinsic role played by the stochastic components of a dynamical system (Van Mourik, Daffertshofer, & Beek, 2006).

On another level of analysis we focused on Detrended Fluctuation Analysis (DFA) as a means to quantify the fractal properties of the fluctuations of the wrist (Peng, Havlin, Stanley, & Goldberger, 1995). The relation between aspects of the changing structure of variation, as expressed by power-law coefficients, and a system's moving closer or farther away from equilibrium in a statistical mechanical sense has been discussed in the literature. For example, a direct relation has been demonstrated between the fractal properties of the distribution function of a dissipative system and both its nonequilibrium steady state and relaxation towards equilibrium (Gilbert, Dòrfman, & Gaspard, 2000). Importantly, such phenomena should not be considered as isolated to physics or physical chemistry. Entropy has also been used as a predictor of the creation of new structure in the face of acquiring a novel cognitive skill (Stephen, Dixon, & Isenhower, in press).

## Method

Seven right-handed participants performed a uni-manual pendulum-swinging task maintaining a steady phase relative to an auditory metronome. They received six trials in each of the three conditions of slow (.67 Hz), resonance (.83 Hz), and fast metronome (1.33 Hz) in a random sequence. The resonant frequency of the wrist-pendulum system was determined following the procedures outlined in Kugler and Turvey (1987) to calculate the period of the simple equivalent pendulum. A goniometer provided measures of wrist deviations (radial and ulnar). Absolute angular displacement furnished the same number of data points per condition for DFA while a peak-extracting algorithm derived trial series of rescaled cycle frequencies serving as the domain of the drift-diffusion analysis.

## Results and Discussion

A repeated-measures ANOVA on the coefficient $Q$ quantifying the stochastic term in the drift-diffusion analysis of frequency entrainment found a significant effect of rate, $F(2, 12) = 5.77$, $p < .05$. A significant quadratic trend, $F(1, 6) = 8.39$, $p < .05$ (Figure 1A), indicates that the noise term is minimal at resonance and increases as pendulum frequencies deviate from resonance. Similar analysis yields a significant effect for the DFA $H$ coefficient, $F(2, 12) = 34.23$, $p < .001$. As Figure 1B shows, $H$ for the fast pace was different from both resonance ($p < .01$) and slow ($p < .01$) but they did not differ from each other ($p = .90$).

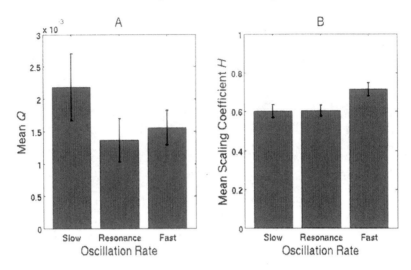

*Figure 1.* Means and standard error bars for the (A) frequency entrainment noise coefficient $Q$ and (B) fluctuation $H$ exponent.

At first blush, these results support our initial hypothesis that variability at non-resonance rates should be special in informative ways. At the level of frequency entrainment, which also can be defined as the amount of the behavioral cycle's deviation from target frequency, noise was augmented by deviation from resonance. A possible interpretation is that maintaining synchrony with the stimulus became harder at these rates. With regard to the noise at the level of wrist motions, the higher $H$ coefficient for fast trials, a signature of more complex fluctuations, can be interpreted in accord with the literature already discussed as indicative of a pendulum swinger being moved farther away from her equilibrium rate. Under such an interpretation, our study is congruent with the hypothesis that one route for a nonlinear system with many degrees of freedom to dissipate excessive stress is to augment its fluctuation complexity.

Our results, however, introduce some ambiguity. Setting aside the quadratic trend in the frequency entrainment noise term, there is no difference between resonance and fast paces ($p > .25$). The pattern is reversed for mean $H$ exponents —there is no difference between slow and resonance. Why did two different patterns characterize two different levels of analysis?

A tentative explanation relies on the conception that state space below and above resonance might allow for different solutions. Drawing the stimulus-human-pendulum system away from resonance induces breaking of symmetry. In the low-rate case the broken symmetry is with respect to cycle duration whereas in the high-rate case the broken symmetry is with respect to increasing complexity of motion as expressed by an increase of the scaling coefficient.

## References

Abarbanel, H. D. I. (1996). *Analysis of chaotic data.* New York, NY: Springer-Verlag.

Amazeen, P. G., Amazeen, E. L., & Turvey, M. T. (1998). Dynamics of human intersegmental coordination: Theory and research. In D. Rosenbaum & C. Collier (Eds.), *Timing of behavior: Neural, computational, and psychological perspectives.* Boston, MA: MIT Press.

Gilbert, T., Dorfman, R., & Gaspard, P. (2000). Entropy production, fractals, and relaxation to equilibrium. *Physical Review Letters, 85(8),* 1606-1609.

Goodman, L., Riley, M. A., Mitra, S., & Turvey, M. T. (2000). Advantages of rhythmic movements at resonance: minimal active degrees of freedom, minimal noise, and maximal predictability. *Journal of Motor Behavior, 32(1),* 3-8.

Kugler, P. N., & Turvey, M. T. (1987). *Information, natural law, and the self-assembly of rhythmic movements.* Hillside, NJ: Erlbaum.

Peng, C.-K., Havlin, S., Stanley, H. E., & Goldberger, A. L. (1995). Quantification of scaling exponentials and crossover phenomena in nonstationary heartbeat time series. *Chaos, 5(1),* 82-87.

Riley, M. A., & Turvey, M. T. (2002). Variability of determinism in motor behavior. *Journal of Motor Behavior, 34(2),* 99-125.

Stephen, D. G., Dixon, J. A., & Isenhower, R. W. (in press). Dynamics of representational change: Entropy, action, and cognition. *Journal of Experimental Psychology: Human Perception and Performance.*

van Mourik, A. M., Daffertshofer, A., & Beek, P. J. (2006). Deterministic and stochastic features of rhythmic human movement. *Biological Cybernetics, 94(3),* 233-244.

*Acknowledgments.* Preparation of this manuscript was supported by a grant from the University of Connecticut Research Foundation.

*Studies in Perception & Action X*
J. B. Wagman & C. C. Pagano (Eds.)
© 2009 Taylor & Francis Group, LLC

# Comparison of Performance of Tray-Carrying Task by Persons with Down Syndrome and Those With Other Forms of Mental Retardation

Shogo Hirata[1], Hideyuki Okuzumi[1], Mitsuru Kokubun[1]
& Masayuki Kumai[2]

[1]Tokyo Gakugei University [2]Tohoku University

This study compares the performance of a tray-carrying task by persons with Down syndrome and those with other forms of mental retardation, and clarifies the features of motor skills execution in persons with Down syndrome. The tray-carrying task is a motor task devised by Kokubun (1999). This task requires subjects to carry a tray bearing a glass filled with water as fast as possible over a distance of 3 meters, but without spilling the water. The time taken and amount of water spilled are measured. Kokubun (1999) compared performance of this task by children with Down syndrome and by children with other forms of mental retardation. The results showed that children with Down syndrome were indeed slower than children with other types of mental retardation, but the amount of water spilled was no different between the two groups. That is to say, while persons with Down syndrome were slow, they were not inaccurate. Although the above findings of Kokubun (1999) have a great impact in changing the general view that persons with Down syndrome were 'clumsy', few studies have been conducted from this perspective. In this study, we conducted the same motor task to confirm the findings of Kokubun (1999), and we conducted a normal walking task to compare to the performance of the tray-carrying task.

## Method

Thirteen persons with Down syndrome (7 males, 6 females) aged 14 to 48 years (29 ± 11.8 years) and 13 persons with other forms of mental retardation (6 males, 7 females) aged 13 to 48 years (29 ± 11.0 years) without sensory and motor impairments were used as subjects. In this study, subjects with Down syndrome were diagnosed by medical doctors, and no one with Autism was included in the group with other forms of mental retardation.

For the tray-carrying task, subjects were given a tray with a glass (9 cm height, 7 cm diameter at the top, 4.5 cm at the bottom, and a capacity of 225 ml) filled with of 200 ml water at the start line and instructed to carry it to a goal line 3 m away as fast as they could without spilling it. The time to reach the goal line was measured with a stop watch. The amount of water remaining in the glass on completion of the task was measured with a measuring cylinder, and this value was subtracted from 200 (ml) to calculate the amount of water spilled. The average of two trials was used as the representative value for that subject. In normal walking, subjects were requested to walk normally for 3 m to compare to the performance of the tray-carrying task. The time was measured. In addition, the adjustment ratio (the time of the tray-carrying task divided by that of normal walking) was also calculated.

## Results and Discussion

Table 1 summarizes the mean (M) and standard deviation (SD) of each of the measures for both groups.

Table 1. Tray-carrying performance by group

| | Tray-carrying task | | | | Normal walking, sec | | Adjustment ratio | |
|---|---|---|---|---|---|---|---|---|
| | Time, sec | | Amount of water spilled, ml | | | | | |
| | M | SD | M | SD | M | SD | M | SD |
| Down Syndrome | 7.98 | 4.04 | 0.08 | 0.28 | 4.26 | 1.21 | 1.97 | 1.14 |
| Mental retardation | 6.54 | 2.53 | 1.08 | 1.55 | 4.60 | 2.27 | 1.52 | 0.43 |

Persons with Down syndrome took more time to complete the task than those with other forms of mental retardation. However, the time required for the normal walking task did not differ between the groups. Persons with Down syndrome spilled less water than the others. Although the adjustment ratio of persons with Down syndrome was larger than that of the others, a 2 (Subject: Down Syndrome vs. Mental Retardation) $\times 2$ (Task condition: tray-carrying vs. normal walking) analysis of variance (ANOVA) yielded no significant differences between the groups ($F_{1, 24}$=0.40, p>.05), but did yield significant differences between the task conditions ($F_{1, 24}$=21.97, p<.05). The interaction was not significant ($F_{1, 24}$=2.16, p>.05). In the amount of water spilled and adjustment ratio, a one-way (subject group) ANOVA yielded significant differences only in the spillage (water: $F_{1, 24}$=5.23, p<.05. ratio: $F_{1, 24}$=1.61, p>.05).

In normal walking, persons with Down syndrome perform at the same speed as those with other forms of mental retardation. But, in the tray-carrying task, persons with Down syndrome tend to take more time than for their normal walking, and behave more cautiously and accurately than people with other forms of retardation. These results accord with the findings of Kokubun (1999). In recent years, Latash (2008) suggested that persons with Down syndrome do not have major qualitative deficits in their motor control mechanisms, and that their clumsy movement was a product of an adaptive strategy to compensate for their delayed decision-making or cerebellar dysfunction. His views are consistent with the results in our study. Bernstein (1996) acutely pointed out 'a demand for dexterity is not in the movements themselves but in the surrounding conditions.' In further investigation, we would like to examine the ecological reality of 'tray-carrying' for persons with Down syndrome and those with other forms of mental retardation using various task conditions (i.e., the size of the glass or amount of water were changed). In our short study, we cannot consider the effect of the subject's intelligence level on task performance. We will address this issue in another article.

### References

Bernstein, N. A. (1966). *On Dexterity and Its Development*. Mahwah, NJ: Lawrence Erlbaum Associates.

Kokubun, M. (1999). Are children with Down syndrome less careful in performing a tray-carrying task than children with other types of mental retardation? *Perceptual and Motor Skills*, 88, 1173-1176.

Latash, M. L. (2008). *Neurophysiological Basis of Movement (Second Edition)*. Champain, IL: Human Kinetics.

*Acknowledgements.* The authors would like to thank the participants who made this work possible.

*Studies in Perception & Action X*
J. B. Wagman & C. C. Pagano (Eds.)
© 2009 Taylor & Francis Group, LLC

# Observation of Action Slips in a Young Child

## Naoya Hirose

Kyoto Notre Dame University

This study investigated a child's action slips during acquisition of a new daily skill. Action slips are the errors that occur when people do an action that is not intended. This study differs in two respects from previous studies on action slips (e.g., Norman, 1981; Reason, 1984). One difference is that we observed a young child instead of adults. Most studies on action slips have been conducted with adults, and little attention has been devoted to children's slips up to now. Developmental research is needed to elucidate the nature of action slips. To the best of our knowledge, this is the first study to report the child's action slips in a daily setting.

The other difference from previous studies is that whereas most studies on action slips have employed the diary method, this study did not. There are several difficulties in the diary method. For example, Reason (1984) argued that, in diary studies, there are at least three kinds of biases (volunteer bias, selection bias, and recording bias). In addition, it is almost impossible for children to keep diaries for their action slips. Thereby, we used video recordings instead of diaries.

It is often pointed out that diary studies underestimate the frequency of slips. People often miss writing down slight slips in their diary, whereas video recoding method can record all of them. Thus, the method can obtain a more accurate count of the frequency of slips. Additionally, it can eliminate the selection and recording biases.

In this study, we coded microslips as well as action slips. Microslips are subtle miscues that occur in manipulation tasks (Reed, Palmer, & Schoenherr, 2009). We identified action slips and microslips according to Hirose's (2007) coding scheme. We first defined the basic units of action and described sequences of action by using these units. Then we identified slips as deviations from the normal sequence, and discriminated between action slips and microlips. Action slips are deviations across multiple basic units, whereas microslips are within one basic unit. Consequently, our definition of slips is rather wider than the previous studies on action slips.

To explore the developmental nature of action slips, we observed a child's mouth rinsing activity during toothbrushing. We chose this behavior because we found frequent action slips in the preliminary observations. In addition, the recording was easy to accomplish because the activity occurred in the same place at around the same time.

**Method**

The only participant of this study was a 4-year-old girl. Her mouth rinsing activities during toothbrushing after dinner were observed for 4 months (from 4:0 to 4:4). Her daily routine of toothbrushing was as follows: First, she brushed her teeth by herself. Second, her parent thoroughly brushed them again. Finally, she rinsed her mouth by herself. She was able to rinse her mouth by herself a few weeks before the time when the study began.

In order to record her mouth rinsing activities, a network camera (AXIS 207W) was installed at the side of a washstand in her house. Video recordings were done automatically by using the motion detection function built in the recording system. All video files were saved to a PC connected to the network. Video files including the participant's mouth rinsing activities were selected to be analyzed. The recording system was always in operation through the period of study, but the target activities were occasionally not recorded due to malfunction of the system or the participant's absence from home. Thus, we obtained 95 day's video files for analysis.

**Results and Discussion**

In the first analysis, we derived a "modal route" (Joe, Ferraro, & Schwartz, 2002) of the mouth rinsing activity without any slips. The route was as follows: ascend step; take cup; hold cup under tap; turn on tap; turn off tap; sip water; swish water around in mouth; spit water; empty cup; put down cup; descend step; wipe mouth with towel. We identified any deviations from this route as slips. Then, we divided these slips into action slips and microslips according to the aforementioned criteria. A series of slips was counted as one action slip or microslip, and those slips that included both action slips and microslips were coded as one action slip. The analysis yielded a total of 62 slips.

Next, we classified slips into five types according to the previous studies of action slips. However, some microslips that could not be categorized into these types were labeled as others. Results of this classification are shown in Table 1. Captures were the most frequent type, accounting for 45.2% of all slips.

*Capture.* Another activity may capture control of the intended activity. The participant often veered from the hand washing activity.

*Redoing.* Repeated actions that need no repetition in the normal situation. The participant turned on the tap twice.

*Anticipation.* Skip a necessary action and perform the next step. The participant turned on the tap before holding the cup under it.

*Sequential.* Sequential errors other than anticipations. The participant attempted to pick up the cup in an inappropriate situation.

*Hesitation.* Common microslips including small pauses during movement. The participant suddenly stopped reaching for the cup, and then resumed reaching.

Finally, we examined developmental changes in slips by dividing the period of study into halves (Figure 1). As shown in Figure 1, action slips decreased drastically in the second half. This suggests that the participant rapidly acquired the skill of mouth rinsing. In contrast, microslips decreased slightly, suggesting that microslips may continue through the time period.

In concluding, we should note that diary studies substantially underestimate the frequency of action slips, estimating one per day at most (Jonsdottir, Adolfsdottir, Cortez, Gunnarsdottir, & Gustafsdottir, 2007). It seems surprising that, in this study, we found a number of slips during a relatively brief activity. Diary method reveals cognition after action, whereas video recording method reveals cognition in action. Future research on slips should focus on cognition in action (Reed, Montgomery, Palmer, & Pittenger, 1995).

*Table 1.* Frequencies of different types of action slips and microslips.

| Type | Action Slips | Microslips |
|---|---|---|
| Capture | 6 | 22 |
| Redoing | 5 | 4 |
| Anticipation | 3 | 4 |
| Sequential | 1 | 4 |
| Hesitation | 0 | 5 |
| Other | 1 | 7 |
| Total | 16 | 46 |

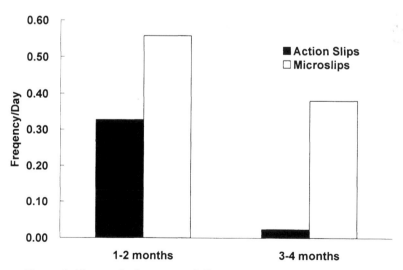

*Figure 1.* Changes in frequency of slip occurrence per day during the period of study.

## References

Hirose, N. (2007). Towards a new taxonomy of microslips. In S. Cummins-Sebree, M. A. Riley & K. Shockley (Eds.), *Studies in perception and action IX.* (pp. 91-94). Mahwah, NJ: Lawrence Erlbaum Associates.

Joe, W. Q., Ferraro, M., & Schwartz, M. F. (2002). Sequencing and interleaving in routine action production. *Neurocase, 8,* 135-150.

Jonsdottir, M. K., Adolfsdottir, S., Cortez, R. D., Gunnarsdottir, M., & Gustafsdottir, A. H. (2007). A diary study of action slips in healthy individuals. *Clinical Neuropsychologist, 21,* 875-883.

Norman, D. A. (1981). Categorization of action slips. *Psychological Review, 88,* 1-15.

Reason, J. T. (1984). Lapses of attention in everyday life. In R. Parasuraman & D. R. Davies (Eds.), *Varieties of attention* (pp. 515-549). Orlando, FL: Academic Press.

Reed, E. S., Montgomery, M., Palmer, C., & Pittenger, J. (1995). Method for studying the invariant knowledge structure of action: Conceptual organization of an everyday action. *American Journal of Psychology, 108,* 37-65.

Reed, E. S., Palmer, C. F., & Schoenherr, D. (2009). On the nature and significance of microslips in everyday activities. *Journal of Ecological Psychology, 4,* 51-66.

*Studies in Perception & Action X*
J. B. Wagman & C. C. Pagano (Eds.)
© 2009 Taylor & Francis Group, LLC

# Relationship Between Attention and Stepping

Yoshifumi Ikeda, Shogo Hirata, Hideyuki Okuzumi,
& Mitsuru Kokubun

Tokyo Gakugei University

Attention when walking was examined in a study that measured reaction time (RT) on a probe-reaction task performed while walking on a treadmill (Kurosawa, 1994). This study concluded that the speed of treadmill walking at which RT minimized approximated the speed of a preferred gait, and that the faster or slower the walking speed, the longer RT became. According to a dynamical systems approach (Hoyt & Taylor, 1981), the stability of system coordination is higher in the optimal mode of walking, that is, the burden of a preferred gait on attention is essentially lower than any other speed of walking. It is, therefore, well supported that RT on a probe-reaction task could minimize at a preferred gait in the study by Kurosawa (1994). Although this finding is quite interesting, there are few other studies that concluded similarly. Therefore, this study examines stepping, an analogy of walking, and the relation between the stability of the motor system and attention by assigning a probe-reaction task and the Stroop test (Stroop, 1935) while in synchronized stepping under various rhythm conditions.

## Method

A total of 10 adults (4 male, 6 female) from 17 to 29 years of age (22.90±2.88 years) participated in this study. Subjects were to perform a probe-reaction task and the Stroop test, which are cognitive tasks to assess attention, while in synchronized stepping under five rhythm conditions of 0.5 Hz, 1.0 Hz, 2.0 Hz, 3.0 Hz, and 4.0 Hz at a fixed place. A metronome was used to make sounds informing subjects of the rhythms. In a probe-reaction (Probe) task which used black rectangular patches as stimuli, subjects named the color of the black patches presented sequentially. The Stroop test was composed of two tasks: a color naming (CN) task, in which subjects named the color of patches in red, blue, green, or yellow presented in a random order; an incongruent color naming (ICN) task, in which subjects named the color of words printed in incongruent colors presented in a random order. In ICN task, stimuli were four words ('red', 'blue', 'yellow', and 'green') printed in a non-matching color of the same four colors. All the stimuli of Probe, CN, and ICN tasks were presented in the white-screened monitor in front of subjects and the reaction time (msec) between presentations of stimuli and oral responses in a microphone was measured by Super Lab (Cedrus®). The mean time of 8 trials for Probe, CN, and ICN tasks in each stepping rhythm condition were used as representative subject variables.

### Results and Discussion

Figure 1 shows the mean of RT on Probe, CN, and ICN tasks for each stepping rhythm condition. Figure 2 shows logarithmic Hz and RT placed on the horizontal axis and vertical axis, respectively. In both figures, the decisive coefficient of the retrogressive curve was broadly high in Probe, CN, and ICN tasks. For Probe, CN, and ICN tasks, the RT minimized at 2.0 Hz and extended whether the Hz was higher or lower. Therefore, in any cognitive tasks, the change of RT between each rhythm condition showed a U-shaped curve whose trough was around 2.0 Hz. In other words, the low burden on attention occurred when stepping around 2.0 Hz. Since it has been already clarified that changes of height and the interval of stepping while performing minimize when stepping around 2.0 Hz (Kamiyama et al; submitted), the coordination and stability of stepping at 2.0 Hz can be even higher. Thus, it follows that a similar conclusion to Kurosawa (1994) applies for stepping as well.

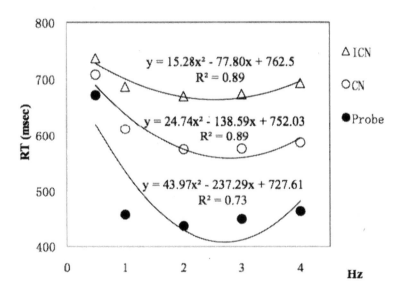

*Figure 1.* Mean reaction time of cognitive tasks at each stepping rhythm.

A two-way ANOVA (within subjects) demonstrated significant effects of the cognitive task-factor ($F_{2,18}$= 65.990, p<.001), the stepping rhythm-factor ($F_{4,36}$= 44.749, p<.001) and interaction effects between the cognitive task-factor and the stepping rhythm-factor ($F_{8,72}$= 4.793, p<.001). The significant interaction effects suggest that the effect of rhythm conditions will not be uniform for each cognitive task. Apparent from the relation between cognitive tasks, RT on the Probe task was shorter than RT on the CN task, and RT on the CN task was shorter than the ICN task in any rhythm condition, which would be affected by the difference in difficulty. However, the change of RT between rhythm conditions in the ICN task, which is thought to be the most difficult cognitive task, was less distinct than that of the other two tasks. That is, the ICN task in the Stroop test has a constant difficulty as a cognitive task irrespective of the stability of stepping. This is more than a little paradoxical considering the greater changes in RT between rhythm conditions in the Probe and CN tasks, which are thought to be less difficult. On the other hand, from figure 1, the extension of RT was not uniform whether it was in the higher or lower Hz with 2.0 Hz centered. This suggests that the burdens of stepping at higher and lower Hz are different from one another. The relation between the stability of stepping and the performance on cognitive tasks has to be discussed in more detail in another article.

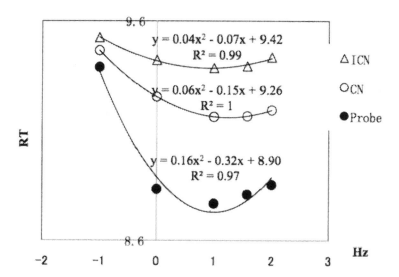

*Figure 2.* Mean reaction time of cognitive tasks at each stepping rhythm (Logarithm).

**References**

Hoyt, D. & Taylor, C. (1981). Gait and the energetics of locomotion in horses. *Nature*, 292, 239-240.

Kurosawa, K. (1994). Evaluation of locomotion efficiency by Probe-reaction time during treadmill walking at various speed and cadence. *Journal of Kyorin Medical Society*, 25, 527-536. (In Japanese with English abstract.)

Stroop, J. R. (1935). Studies of interference in serial verbal reactions. *Journal of Experimental Psychology*, 18, 643-662.

*Acknowledgements.* The authors would like to thank the participants who made this work possible.

*Studies in Perception & Action X*
J. B. Wagman & C. C. Pagano (Eds.)

# Relationship Between Stepping and its Tempo

Yu Kamiyama, Shogo Hirata, Hideyuki Okuzumi,
& Mitsuru Kokubun

Tokyo Gakugei University

In recent years, many studies of reciprocal movement have been conducted using the dynamical systems approach (Kelso, 1995). There are many kinds of reciprocal movements. Sekiya et al, (1996) focused on the human gait, which is a representative reciprocal movement, and clarified that whether the walking speed is fast or slow, the variability of elements, such as increasing step length or step rate, may increase and lead to a breakdown of gait stability. Although the above findings of Sekiya et al, (1996) are very interesting, few studies have been conducted on reciprocal movements from this viewpoint. In this study, we investigate the relationship between stepping and its tempo. A synchronized stepping movement is a similar movement to the human gait.

## Method

The subjects were 30 healthy adults (15 males, 15 females) aged 20 to 29 years (22.81±1.70 years). In this study, the subjects stepping movement was recorded by a position sensor (C2399, Hamamatsu Photonics, Japan), consisting of a camera and amplifier which could record the track trajectory of an LED from a distance. The track of the LED is output laterally and sagittally. These two analog signals were input to a personal computer though an A/D conversion board at a sampling frequency of 100 Hz and recorded on a hard disk. Subjects stand up on a flat floor wearing low-heeled shoes or thin socks and a right ankle band to which the LED was attached, and were asked to step according to a sound. Sound stimuli were presented by electronic metronome, and the sounds continued while stepping. In this study, we presented five rhythm tempos such as 0.5 Hz, 1 Hz, 2 Hz, 3 Hz and 4 Hz, which were randomized for each person. Finally, subjects were asked to step naturally without the rhythm sounds at a preferred tempo.

Using the recorded digital data, we calculated the ten values of step time (ms) and step height (cm) at each rhythm tempo. Then, the average values (step time, step height) and coefficients of variation (time CV, height CV) were calculated for each person. Step time is defined as the average rhythm in the stepping movement, and can be used as index of whether the subject stepping is synchronized with the presented stimulus. Step height is an index that shows the maximum movement amplitude in the vertical direction in right leg. The time CV and height CV can be used as an index of step time variability and step height variability. If these two values are large, the variability of step time or step height is high, and the stability of stepping is low.

## Results and Discussion

Table 1 summarizes the mean (M) and standard deviation (SD) of each measurement at each rhythm tempo. In this study, we only measure the right leg movement by the position of the sensor. Thus, the step time's theoretical value was the time for two iterations of stimulus sound at the each rhythm tempo, such as 0.5 Hz = 4000 ms, 1 Hz = 2000 ms, 2 Hz = 1000 ms, 3 Hz = 667 ms, and 4 Hz = 500 ms.

Table 1. Mean (M) and standard deviation (SD) of each variable at each rhythm tempo

| Rhythm tempo | Step time (ms) | | Step height (cm) | | Time CV | | Height CV | |
|---|---|---|---|---|---|---|---|---|
| | M | SD | M | SD | M | SD | M | SD |
| 0.5Hz | 4001.17 | 26.09 | 14.78 | 7.17 | 0.05 | 0.02 | 0.18 | 0.11 |
| 1Hz | 1994.83 | 12.83 | 14.51 | 6.48 | 0.04 | 0.02 | 0.14 | 0.05 |
| 2Hz | 1000.00 | 5.25 | 9.17 | 4.42 | 0.04 | 0.01 | 0.12 | 0.04 |
| 3Hz | 668.50 | 7.67 | 5.63 | 2.85 | 0.06 | 0.02 | 0.15 | 0.05 |
| 4Hz | 505.67 | 7.76 | 4.63 | 2.23 | 0.08 | 0.02 | 0.17 | 0.06 |
| Prefer | 1107.00 | 188.82 | 10.12 | 5.46 | 0.04 | 0.02 | 0.11 | 0.05 |

The results show that the step times correspond to the theoretical value at each rhythm tempo. Moreover, the preferred tempo approximates the values at 2 Hz. Step height rises significantly with the slowing of the tempo ($F_{5, 145} = 54.2, p < .01$). Time CV becomes larger when the tempo is slower or faster, and it is a minimum at 1 Hz and 2 Hz ($F_{5, 145} = 27.7, p < .01$). The height CV also becomes larger when the tempo is slower or faster, and it is a minimum at 2 Hz ($F_{5, 145} = 7.3, p < .01$). The change of each CV between each rhythm tempo formed a U-shaped curve whose trough was around 2 Hz. Each CV of the preferred tempo was small, and the stability of preferred stepping was very high.

Results in this study were as follows. First, step time strongly correlates to step height. This relationship between step time and step height suggests the possibility that one synergy (Bernstein, 1996) was formed in stepping. Second, in the vicinity of 2 Hz tempo, temporal stepping stability and spatial stepping stability were very high, whereas, when the rhythm tempo became faster or slow than 2 Hz, there was a breakdown of stepping stability. These results accord with the findings of Sekiya et al. (1996). In this study, we could say that the stability of preferred stepping was very high. In further studies, we will have to examine various-aged children's performance to investigate the developmental process of stability of stepping.

## References

Bernstein, N. A. (1966). *On Dexterity and Its Development*. Mahwah, NJ: Lawrence Erlbaum Associates.

Kelso, J. A. S. (1995). *Dynamic Pattens*. Cambridge, MA: The MIT press.

Sekiya, N., Nagasaki, H., Ito, H., Furuna, T (1996). The invariant relationship between step length and step rate during free walking, *Journal of Human Movement Studies*, 30, 241-257. (In Japanese with English abstract.)

*Acknowledgements.* The authors would like to thank the participants who made this work possible.

*Studies in Perception & Action X*
J. B. Wagman & C. C. Pagano (Eds.)
© 2009 Taylor & Francis Group, LLC

# Dynamics of Motor Performance in Visually Guided Force Production

Nikita A. Kuznetsov & Michael A. Riley

Perceptual-Motor Dynamics Laboratory, Department of Psychology,
University of Cincinnati

The structure of motor variability is informative about underlying motor control processes (Riley & Turvey, 2002; Slifkin & Newell, 1999). The presence of structured (non-random) fluctuations in movement is thought to indicate a capacity for greater behavioral flexibility and greater overall adaptability to novel situations compared to systems that do not exhibit this pattern of fluctuation. In this study we examined the structure of variability of single-digit force production in regard to the use of adaptive motor control strategies.

Producing a specified level of force could be achieved using two general strategies. The first involves anticipatory modulations of force in order to keep current performance within criterion levels. This is possible if the frequency of visual feedback is high and the task goal is known, conditions that are known to facilitate performance (Sosnoff & Newell, 2005). The second strategy involves utilizing feedback in a reactive, rather than prospective, fashion—force corrections are made only after the force criterion is violated. This strategy is expected when information that permits prospective control is absent.

The goal of this study was to determine the relation of the structure of force fluctuations to prospective and reactive force control strategies. Participants produced a specified force under manipulations of visual information about performance. A continuous display, which was designed to encourage prospective control, indicated the current level of force in relation to the goal and to the boundaries of an acceptable range around the goal. A discrete feedback display, which was designed to elicit a reactive strategy, only signalled when (and in which direction) the current level of force deviated from the acceptable range. Prospective control in the continuous condition was expected to yield smoother changes in force values. In contrast, the reactive changes in force based on discrete feedback were expected to yield discontinuous force time series containing occasional irregularities due to rapid force readjustments enacted when feedback was presented. These structural differences in the force signals were quantified using the *%LAM* measure from recurrence quantification analysis (RQA; Marwan, 2002; Weber & Zbilut, 2005). *%LAM* is the percentage of recurrent points forming vertical lines in the recurrence plot. Signals with more discontinuities exhibit a greater number of laminar states (and hence greater %*LAM*) than more smooth, continuous signals.

## Method

Eleven right-handed University of Cincinnati undergraduates participated for course credit. Participants attempted to produce a constant level of force (20% of the participant's maximum; mean maximum force was $37.1 \pm 8.7$ N) with two different kinds of displays (continuous vs. discrete) and three levels of difficulty (allowed force variability of 1, 5, and 10% of the target level). There were 4 trials in each condition (24 trials total), each lasting 30 seconds, presented in random order. Force was recorded at 100 Hz using a Bertec (Worthington, OH) load cell. Unfiltered forces normal to the load cell surface were analyzed.

Participants sat at a table with the load cell mounted on it, 40 cm away from a monitor positioned at eye height. In the continuous display condition, the goal force was indicated by a gray band on the display spanning the minimum and maximum levels of allowed force. Current force was indicated in real time by a red dot. Participants tried to maintain the dot within the band. They could always see how the force they were producing related to the goal level.

In the discrete display condition participants were asked to produce the same levels of force, but the red dot only took three possible discrete, static values: above, within, or below the band, indicating, respectively, that force exceeded, matched (within limits), or was less than the goal force. Force was measured in real time but the dot position did not change unless force changed from one of those three states to another. .

RQA was conducted using $d = 3$, $\tau = 20$, and a variable radius calculated as a percentage of the mean distance between time-delayed vectors of force values. Radius was adjusted to achieve %*REC* = $1 \pm 0.2$ for each trial. Two consecutive vertical points defined a vertical line. The first 4 seconds of the trial were discarded to omit transients.

## Results and Discussion

Figure 1 shows sample force time series and corresponding recurrence plots. The percentage of sampled force values within the allowed limits (accuracy) and %*LAM* were calculated for each trial and averaged over trials in each condition. These averaged values were submitted to separate 2 (display: continuous vs. discrete) × 3 (difficulty: 1, 5, and 10% of target force level) repeated-measures ANOVAs.

There was a main effect of difficulty on accuracy, $F(2, 22) = 990.76$, $p < .0001$, $\eta_p^2 = .99$. Participants were least successful in the 1% condition followed by the 5% and 10% conditions (Figure 2, left). Participants performed better with the continuous displays than the discrete ones, $F(1, 22) = 49.32$, $p < .0001$, $\eta_p^2 = .82$—it was harder to maintain the required level of force using discrete feedback. The difficulty × display interaction approached but did not reach significance, $F(2, 22) = 3.34$, $p = .054$, $\eta_p^2 = .23$.

Discrete displays led to higher *%LAM* than continuous displays, $F(1, 22) = 102.68$, $p < .0001$, $\eta_p^2 = .90$ (Figure 2, right). This indicates a greater tendency for discontinuous irregularities in the force time series in the discrete display condition, and suggests that *%LAM* can be used to measure differences between the qualitatively different motor control strategies encouraged by these display conditions. Difficulty did not have an effect on *%LAM*,($p = .09$, $\eta_p^2 = .20$), and although differences between the two kinds of display conditions were more pronounced in the most difficult (1% range) condition there was no difficulty × display type interaction ($p = .42$, $\eta_p^2 = .08$). Future research will focus on identifying critical values of feedback characteristics that elicit qualitative shifts in isometric force production strategies.

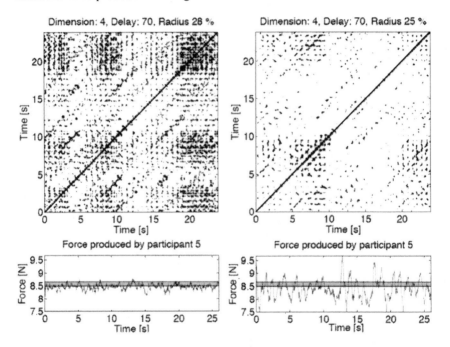

*Figure 1.* Time series (bottom) of force produced in the 1% continuous (left panel) and 1% discrete (right panel) displays and (top) their corresponding recurrence plots. *%LAM* is 63% in the continuous condition and 94% in the discrete condition.

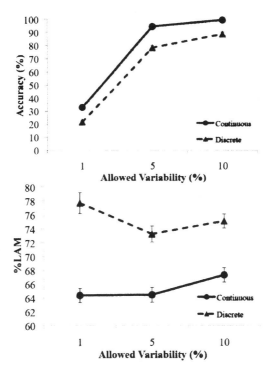

*Figure 2.* Average values of accuracy (left) and %LAM (right). Error bars indicate one standard error.

## References

Marwan, N., Wessel, N., Meyerfeldt, U., Schirdewan, A., & Kurths, J. (2002). Recurrence-plot-based measures of complexity and their application to heart-rate-variability data. *Physical Review E, 66*, 026702-026702.

Riley, M. A., & Turvey, M. T. (2002). Variability and determinism in motor behavior. *Journal of Motor Behavior, 34*, 99-125.

Slifkin, A. B., & Newell, K. M. (1999). Noise, information transmission, and force variability. *Journal Of Experimental Psychology: Human Perception & Performance, 25*, 837-851.

Sosnoff, J. J., Newell, K. M. (2005). Intermittent visual information and the multiple timescales of visual motor control of continuous isometric force production. *Perception & Psychophysics, 67*, 335–344.

Webber, C. L., & Zbilut, J. P. (2005). Recurrence quantification analysis of nonlinear dynamical systems. In M. A. Riley & G. C. Van Orden (Eds.), *Tutorials in contemporary nonlinear methods for the behavioral sciences* (pp. 26-95). Retrieved October 27, 2008, from http://www.nsf.gov/sbe/bcs/pac/nmbs/nmbs.jsp.

*Studies in Perception & Action X*
J. B. Wagman & C. C. Pagano (Eds.)
© 2009 Taylor & Francis Group, LLC

# Microslips in a Manual Placing Task

## Ken Yoshida & Thomas A. Stoffregen

University of Minnesota

Microlips are small glitches that occur in manual action. Previous research has documented the existence of microslips in adults and children (e.g., Reed & Schoenherr, 1992, Suzuki & Sasaki, 2001). These authors argued that microslips occur during transitions between one action to another. Suzuki & Sasaki manipulated the complexity of the task situation (e.g., the presence or absence of distracter elements) and found that microslips were more common in more complex task situations.

The task complexity manipulations of Suzuki and Sasaki (2001) were qualitative. We attempted to develop a method in which the frequency of microslips could be related to quantitative manipulation of a control parameter. We examined two preferred modes in manual, pronation and supination. Preferred modes of action have been widely studied including grip configuration (Cesari & Newell, 1999), intra- and inter-personal grasping (Richardson, et al., 2007), and bimanual finger coordination (Kelso, 1984). We asked participants to grasp a wooden rod and place it upright on a table. To do this, they were obliged to choose between pronate and supinate hand posture in grasping the rod. We varied the initial position of the rod, in terms of its angle relative to the participant. We hypothesized that the occurrence of pronatory or supinatory reaching would be influenced by the angle of the rod, and that at some critical angle there would be a reliable boundary between pronate and supinate reaching. We expected microslips to occur as participants prepared to grasp the rod, and we predicted that microslips would be more common when the rod angle was near the transition between pronate and supinate reaching modes.

### Method

Twenty-one undergraduate students participated. The experimental protocol was reviewed and approval by the institutional review board of the University of Minnesota.

Participants sat in front of the table, with a rod presentation device on either side (Figure 1). The angle of rod was varied, in 15° increments, from -15° to

90°. Participants were asked to pull the rod from the rod-base and place it vertically on the table in front of them. There were 80 trials per participant (40 for each hand), which were video recorded.

Frequencies of pronation/supination reaching and microslips were coded from the video files. In addition, microslips were categorized using the classification of Reed and Schoenherr (1992). The categories were *hesitations*, *trajectory changes*, *touches*, and *hand shape changes*.

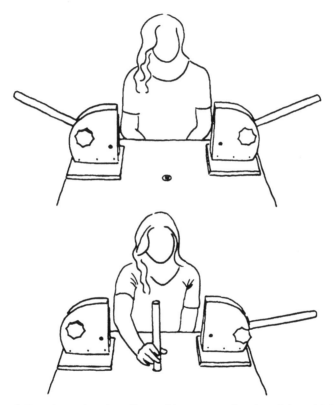

*Figure 1.* Experimental setting. Two rod-bases were placed on right and left sides of the table. Angles of rod were adjustable with 15° increments. Participants were instructed to lift and place the rod on the target which was marked on the table.

**Results and Discussion**

Contrary to our expectation, rod angle had only a weak effect on pronation/supination. This was because participants elected to use supination in 99.9% of cases when reaching for the rod. The rare pronate reaches tended to occur when the rod angle was -15°. Thus, we were not able to test our prediction that microslips would occur near pronation/supination transitions. There were a total of seven microslips in the reach/grasp phase. Six of these were touches, and one was a hand shape change.

Our analysis revealed that microslips were more common in the terminal part of the action, when participants were preparing to place the rod on the table. We observed 29 hesitations during rod placement. This result indicates that microslips can occur in relatively simple situations.

Reed and Schoenherr (1992) argued that microslips should tend to occur near transitions of action modes. This insight inspired our attempt to develop a method in which the frequency of microslip occurrence would be related to quantitative manipulation of a control parameter that was related to a transition between two action modes. We developed a grasp-and-place task in which participants were required to choose between pronation and supination of the hand when reaching for the to-be-grasped object. The utility of our method depended upon the occurrence of a transition between pronation and supination. We found some evidence of a transition between reaching modes, but this evidence occurred only at one of the extreme values of our control parameter. In future research, we will attempt to identify values of a control parameter that can reliably lead to transitions between action modes in reaching.

## References

Cesari, P., & Newell, K. M. (1999). The scaling of human grip configurations. *Journal of Experimental Psychology: Human Perception and Performance*, 25, 927-935.

Kelso, J. A. S. (1984) Phase transitions and critical behavior in human bimanual coordination. *American Jounral o Physiology: Regulatory, Intergrative and Comparative*, 15, R1000-R1004.

Reed, E. S., & Schoenherr, D. (1992). The neuropathology of everyday life: On the nature and significance of micro-slips in everyday activities. Unpublished manuscript.

Richardson, M. J., Marsh, K. L, & Baron, R. M. (2007). Judging and actualizing intrapersonal and interpersonal affordances. *Journal of Experimental Psychology: Human Perception and Performance*. 33, 845-859

Suzuki, K., & Sasaki, M. (2001). The task constraints on selection of potential units of action: An Analysis of microslips observed in everyday tasks. *Cognitive Studies*, 8, 121-138.

*Studies in Perception & Action X*
J. B. Wagman & C. C. Pagano (Eds.)
© 2009 Taylor & Francis Group, LLC

# Chapter 2:

# Interpersonal Coordination

*Studies in Perception & Action X*
J. B. Wagman & C. C. Pagano (Eds.)
© 2009 Taylor & Francis Group, LLC

*Studies in Perception & Action X*
J. B. Wagman & C. C. Pagano (Eds.)
© 2009 Taylor & Francis Group, LLC

# Perceiving Affordances for a Dyad

Tehran J. Davis, Michael A. Riley, Kevin Shockley,
Kimberly Capehart, & Justin Fine

Department of Psychology, University of Cincinnati

An affordance is an opportunity for action provided by the environment to an organism. Affordances can often be defined as an environmental property scaled by the action capabilities of an organism. For example, an opening affords passing through for an individual whose widest body dimension (usually the shoulder, $S$) is less than the dimensions of the aperture ($A$). However, not all affordances are relative to individuals. It is often the case that people act together to achieve a shared goal. While considerable attention has been given to how affordances constrain individuals, only recently have a few investigations investigated the affordances of groups of individuals engaged in a joint action. For example, Isenhower and colleagues (2005) demonstrated that people are able to distinguish the boundaries between an affordance for oneself and an affordance for a dyad. The present study extended previous findings regarding affordances and joint actions by determining whether individuals were perceptually sensitive to affordances specific to a dyad of which they were a member.

We investigated the affordance of pass-through-ability of an aperture for both individuals and dyads. In individuals, the affordance for passing through an aperture may be expressed as an intrinsic measure, $A/S$ (see Warren & Whang, 1987). As long as the $A/S$ ratio is above some critical value, individuals can pass through a doorway without needing to rotate their shoulders. Warren and Whang found that this critical $A/S > 1$, reflecting a margin or "safety buffer" to account for the natural lateral body sway that occurs while walking. Experiment 1 determined this critical boundary for dyads.

## Experiment 1

In Experiment 1 we determined the critical $A/S$ value at which both an individual and a dyad could walk through a doorway without rotating their shoulders.

**Method**

Participants (N=7; mean shoulder width = 46.6 cm) were asked to walk through a doorway without touching its perimeter. Starting from 4 m away, in half of the trials, individuals approached the aperture alone. In the other half, participants performed in a dyad, approaching the aperture alongside a model (shoulder width: 47 cm) the entire length of the walk and arriving at the doorway concurrently. Aperture width was varied by trial (by either increasing or reducing width by 5 cm). For individuals the apertures ranged from 40 to 90 cm, and for dyads, from 70 cm to 120 cm.

All trials were recorded by an overhead camera mounted directly above the aperture. Video from each trial was clipped to capture the final 94 cm of the participants' approach. All video clips were later presented in randomized order to five separate raters. The raters identified trials in which the participant (or in instances in which there was a dyad, either the participant or the model) rotated or adjusted their shoulders in order to fit through the aperture. Inter-rater reliability was determined to be acceptably high (0.75 – 0.90).

**Results and Discussion**

$A/S$ was calculated for each trial (in the dyad condition, $S$ was equal to the combined shoulder widths of the participant and the model). From these data, the critical action boundary between turns and no turns, or the point of subjective equality (where raters indicated a turn 50% of the time), was calculated by submitting the percent turn scores at each $A/S$ to a probit function. The points of subjective equality were predicted using the best-fitting probit function. A t-test for independent means comparing the estimated points of subjective equality between individual (M = 1.21) and dyad (M = 1.12) conditions was significant, $t(6) = -4.31$, $p < .01$, such that the critical $A/S$ ratio for dyads was less than individuals walking alone.

The critical $A/S$ for both individuals and dyads indicated the presence of a buffer zone (i.e., $A/S > 1$) in determining pass-through-ability. However, these results suggest that when individuals were engaged in the task together as a dyad, the resulting joint affordance was not the sum of the two individuals' separate affordances. Had this been the case, we would have identified identical critical $A/S$ ratios across individual and dyad conditions. Instead, critical $A/S$ ratios for individuals were greater than for dyads, indicating that the affordance boundary for dyads is under-additive (less than the sum of two individuals' boundaries).

**Experiment 2**

In Experiment 2, we addressed the question of whether or not individuals were perceptually sensitive to the affordance of passing through an aperture for a dyad—specifically, whether observers were sensitive to the under-additivity.

We also determined whether different types of visual experience were equally adequate to support accurate judgments for oneself, a model, and the dyad.

## Method

Participants (N=30) ranged in shoulder width from 36.00 to 50.90 cm (mean = 43.16 ± 3.75 cm.). Prior to data collection, participants were randomly assigned to one of three conditions: 1) *See walk*, the participant stood at the end of a hallway 1.8 m wide and watched a model (from Experiment 1) walk down and back the hallway's length (10.67 m) five times; 2) *Walk with*, the participant walked alongside the model maintaining a constant distance as the two walked the length of the hallway 5 times; 3) *See standing*, the participant only viewed the model standing still for one minute prior to the start of the experiment.

Participants were then led into a laboratory to make estimates. The doorway from Experiment 1 was set up inside a chamber ($3 \times 2 \times 2.5$ m) enclosed by black curtains hanging from the ceiling. The participants were able look into the chamber via a small view port located at eye-level at the corner of one "wall" of curtains. The doorway was positioned inside the chamber 2.25 m from the viewport. The participant and model stood outside the chamber with the model positioned 2 m to the right of the participant, facing perpendicular to the participant at all times.

Participants estimated the minimum aperture width through which they or the dyad could walk (side-by-side in the case of the dyad) without turning the shoulders. Using the method of limits, participants were instructed to inform the experimenter, who was manually moving the doorway, to stop when the doorway reached the perceived critical limit. Two consecutive estimations, corresponding to the two directions of presentation (ascending and descending aperture widths), were averaged together to make a single trial. Type of estimate (self, other, dyad) was presented in counterbalanced blocks of 8 trials for a total of 24 trials. Between trials, participants were instructed to either close their eyes (during the self-judgment condition) or turn to look at the model (during other and for the dyad conditions).

## Results and Discussion

Separate $3 \times 3 \times 8$ ANOVAs were conducted on raw estimates and on estimates scaled to $A/S$. For mean raw estimates, a significant effect was observed for estimate type (self, model, dyad), $F(2,27) = 410.65$, $p < .01$, $\eta_p^2 = .85$. Bonferroni-corrected post-hoc tests showed that raw estimates in all three estimate-type conditions differed significantly from one another ($p < .0167$), increasing in value from estimates for self, to estimates for the model, to estimates for the dyad. No significant trial effect was observed, nor for between group comparisons of task experience.

For mean $A/S$, a significant effect for judgment type was also observed, $F(2,27) = 32.23$, $p < .05$, $\eta_p^2 = .31$. However, post-hoc tests revealed that while mean perceived critical $A/S$ ratios for self (1.14) and model (1.16) did not differ from one another, critical *A/S* for dyads were significantly less than each (*p* > .05) (see Figure 1).

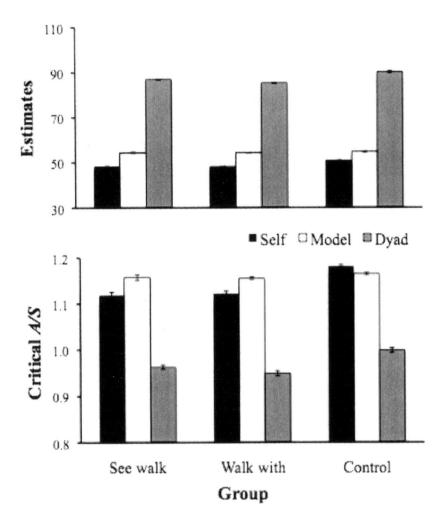

*Figure 1.* Perceptual reports of Experiment 2 expressed as raw data (top) and *A/S* ratios (bottom).

Taken together, these results suggest that while individuals were sensitive to absolute differences between themselves and the model, they scaled affordances for both to the same intrinsically scaled *A/S* values. Furthermore, the critical *A/S* differences between individuals and dyads mirrors the trend from Experiment 1, and indicates that participants were sensitive to the affordance of the dyad.

**References**

Isenhower, R. W., Marsh, K. L., Carello, C., Baron, R. M., & Richardson, M. J. (2005). The specificity of intrapersonal and interpersonal affordance boundaries: Intrinsic versus extrinsic metrics. In H. Heft & K. L. Marsh (Eds.), *Studies in perception and action, viii.* Mahwah, NJ: Erlbaum.

Warren, W. H., & Whang, S. (1987). Visual guidance of walking through apertures: Body-scaled information for affordances. *Journal of Experimental Psychology: Human Perception and Performance, 13*, 371-383.

*Studies in Perception & Action X*
J. B. Wagman & C. C. Pagano (Eds.)
© 2009 Taylor & Francis Group, LLC

# Inter- and Intra-personal Coordination in Autistic and Typically-Developing Children

Robert W. Isenhower[1], Kerry L. Marsh[1], Paula Silva[1],
Michael J. Richardson[2], and R. C. Schmidt[3]

[1]Center for the Ecological Study of Perception and Action,
University of Connecticut
[2]Department of Psychology, Colby College
[3]Department of Psychology, College of the Holy Cross

Autism Spectrum Disorder (ASD) is a pervasive developmental disorder that is currently diagnosed on the basis of a triad of behavioral indicators: (1) deficits in social interaction, (2) deficits in language for communication, and (3) restricted and repetitive interests and activities (*DSM-IV-TR*, 2000). Points (1) and (2) are fundamentally coordinative in nature. Therefore, studying coordination in children with ASD may reveal subtleties of the dynamics of intrapersonal and interpersonal coordination not apparent in typically-developing (TD) children.

Coordinated behavior has been shown to be constrained by a coupled oscillator dynamic and can be described by the so-called HKB equation (Haken, Kelso, & Bunz, 1985):

$$\dot{\phi} = \Delta\omega - a \sin\ \phi - 2b \sin\ 2\phi + \sqrt{Q}\ \zeta$$

Predictions of the HKB equation have found substantial support in a pendulum-swinging paradigm. This is so whether the pendulums are held by a single individual (Kugler & Turvey, 1987) or by two individuals (Schmidt & Turvey, 1994). Moreover, interpersonal coordination is apparent even without explicit instruction to coordinate (Richardson, Marsh, & Schmidt, 2005). Critical to the current study, the HKB equation is not limited to the wrist-pendulum paradigm. The current study uses an interpersonal rocking chair paradigm (cf. Richardson, Marsh, Isenhower, Goodman, & Schmidt, 2007) and an intrapersonal drumming task (cf. Brakke, Fragaszy, Simpson, Hoy, & Cummins-Sebree, 2007) to assess coordination in ASD and TD children.

## Method

Children (ranging from 2.5 to 8 years of age) participated in two tasks: interpersonal rocking and intrapersonal drumming. Out of the total sample of children (N = 23), TD children ($N_{TD}$ = 7) and children with ASD ($N_{ASD}$ = 7) were age-matched based on a battery of standard clinical assessments.

During the interpersonal task child/parent pairs were seated in rocking chairs (Fig. 1, left). Movement data were collected from sensors attached to the chairs. The parent's rocking chair was weighted so that its natural frequency closely matched the natural frequency of the child's rocking chair ($\approx$ 0.83 Hz). A metronome that only the parent could hear was used in order to keep the rocking frequency of the parent constant. This also ensured that any spontaneous coordination observed was due to the child entraining to the parent. Parents read a story to their child in order to keep their attention. Children were never told to rock; however, most children did rock spontaneously.

*Figure 1.* (left) Interpersonal rocking and (right) intrapersonal drumming.

During the intrapersonal task, children were first shown how to hold the drumsticks and how to strike the drum in an in-phase and an anti-phase manner. They were then instructed to strike the drum continuously for two 45 second trials (one in-phase and one anti-phase) at their own preferred pace. The order of the trials was counterbalanced across participants. Movement data were collected from sensors attached to the drumsticks (Fig. 1, right).

## Results and Discussion

For interpersonal rocking, continuous relative phase (CRP) was examined. The amount of time that the child's chair was in a particular phase relation with the parent, in nine steps from 0° (in-phase) to 180° (anti-phase), was assessed for the age-matched sub-sample (N = 14) of the children. A 2 (Group: TD vs. ASD) by 9 (Phase bins) mixed ANOVA revealed a significant Group × Phase bin interaction, $F(8, 96) = 2.57$, $p < .05$, $\eta_p^2 = .18$. The CRP results for the interpersonal rocking task indicate the pattern of coordination observed for TD children is different than the pattern observed for children with ASD. TD children exhibit more in-phase coordination than children with ASD; the latter showed no discernable preferred phase region (Fig. 2, left).

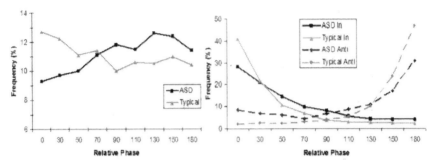

*Figure 2.* (left) Amount of time spent by each group in each of the phase bins. (right) Amount of time spent in the required phase (in- or anti-phase) by the two groups of children.

For intrapersonal drumming, CRP was examined separately for in-phase coordination and for anti-phase coordination using parallel Group × Phase region mixed ANOVAs for the age-matched sub-sample (N = 14). The analyses revealed a significant Group × Phase bin interaction for both. For in-phase coordination, $F(8, 96) = 3.81$, $p < .001$, $\eta_p^2 = .20$, an independent samples t-test found a significant difference between the in-phase bin of the two groups, $t(12) = 2.28$, $p < .05$. For anti-phase coordination, $F(8, 96) = 4.23$, $p < .001$, $\eta_p^2 = .21$, an independent samples t-test found a significant difference between the anti-phase bin of the two groups, $t(12) = 2.59$, $p < .05$. Overall, the CRP analyses of the drumming data revealed significantly more in-phase and anti-phase coordination for TD children than for children with ASD. Typical children are better able to maintain the required phase during drumming (Fig. 2, right).

Cross recurrence quantification (CRQ) analysis was also applied to the rocking and drumming data. CRQ measures the dynamic similarity between two time series embedded in a reconstructed phase space. No significant effects were found for rocking. For drumming, however, differences were apparent. For anti-phase coordination, TD children had significantly greater % recurrence than ASD children, $t(12) = 2.29$, $p < .05$, significantly longer meanline, $t(12) = 3.14$, $p < .05$, and a marginally longer maxline, $t(12) = 1.82$, $p < .08$. For in-phase coordination, in contrast, TD children had a marginally *shorter* meanline than ASD children, $t(12) = 2.12$, $p < .06$. Previous research has shown that for CRQ analysis maxline and meanline are indices of attractor strength and % recurrence is an index of noise (Richardson, Schmidt, & Kay, 2007). Under this analysis, it is possible that typically developing children assemble oscillatory drumming movements that have less noise than children with ASD. However, given that the meanline difference between TD children and children with ASD is the opposite for in-phase coordination and anti-phase coordination, the results concerning attractor strength of the drumming movements are equivocal.

Overall, the results of the current study find coordination differences between children with ASD and TD children for both interpersonal and intrapersonal tasks. Uninstructed interpersonal coordination between parent and child in the rocking task revealed that TD children spent more time in phase with the parent whereas ASD children showed no particular preferred phase relation. For the intrapersonal drumming task, which required maintaining a particular phase relation between their own hands, both groups of children were successful: 0° was produced under the in-phase instruction, 180° was produced under the antiphase instruction. However, TD children were better at maintaining the required phase relation. The results of CRQ analysis indicate that TD children assemble oscillatory movements with less noise than children with ASD, although it is unclear if the attractor strength of the oscillatory movements in either group differs from each other.

### References

American Psychiatric Association. (2000). *Diagnostic and statistical manual of mental disorders: DSM-IV-TR*. Washington, DC: American Psychiatric Press, Inc.

Brakke, K., Fragaszy, D. M., Simpson, K., Hoy, E., & Cummins-Sebree, S. (2007). The production of bimanual percussion in 12- to 24-month old children. *Infant Behavior & Development, 30*, 2-15.

Haken, H., Kelso, J. A. S., & Bunz, H. (1985). A theoretical model of phase transitions in human hand movements. *Biological Cybernetics, 51*, 347-356.

Kugler, P. N., & Turvey, M. T. (1987). *Information, natural law, and the self-assembly of rhythmic movements*. Hillsdale, NJ: Lawrence Erlbaum Associates.

Richardson, M. J., Marsh, K. L., Isenhower, R. W., Goodman, J., & Schmidt, R. C. (2007). Rocking together: Dynamics of intentional and unintentional interpersonal coordination. *Human Movement Science, 26*, 867-891.

Richardson, M. J., Marsh, K. L., & Schmidt, R. C. (2005). Effects of visual and verbal information on unintentional interpersonal coordination. *Journal of Experimental Psychology: Human Perception and Performance, 31*, 62-79.

Richardson, M. J., Schmidt, R. C., & Kay, B. A. (2007). Distinguishing the noise and attractor strength of coordinated limb movements using recurrence analysis. *Biological Cybernetics, 96*, 59-78.

Schmidt, R. C., & Turvey, M. T. (1994). Phase-entrainment dynamics of visually coupled rhythmic movements. *Biological Cybernetics, 70*, 369-376.

*Acknowledgements.* This research was supported by a Cure Autism Now (CAN) Grant and a National Science Foundation Grant # 0240277.

*Studies in Perception & Action X*
J. B. Wagman & C. C. Pagano (Eds.)
© 2009 Taylor & Francis Group, LLC

# The Influence of Interpersonal Interaction on Postural Coordination Dynamics in a Suprapostural Task

Manuel Varlet, Ludovic Marin, Julien Lagarde, & Benoît G. Bardy

Efficiency and Deficiency Laboratory, University Montpellier1, Montpellier, France

Previous postural coordination studies have shown that multi-segment postural coordination can be described by the relative phase between the ankle and hip in a suprapostural task (i.e., when posture is investigated within a goal-directed task; Bardy, Marin, Stoffregen, & Bootsma, 1999). Research revealed that when participants "posturaly" track the sinusoidal motion of a target, two stable patterns emerge from the ankle-hip relative phase: an in-phase mode (close to 20°) for low target frequency displacements and an anti-phase mode (180°) for high target frequency motions. Increasing target frequency produced an abrupt change from in-phase to anti-phase coordination and inversely, decreasing frequency produced a change from anti-phase to in-phase coordination (Bardy, Oullier, Bootsma, & Stoffregen, 2002).

For a decade, studies have been investigating postural coordination when participants were alone and almost none have examined posture in interpersonal situations. In our everyday life, however, posture it is not an end in itself, but rather it is often used to (involuntarily) communicate, work with someone, practice a sport and so on. Shockley, Santana and Fowler (2003) have shown objective evidence of postural influence in interpersonal situation. However, this study only measured a global assessment of postural activity and did not investigate the postural coordination of paired participants. The goal of the current study, therefore, was to investigate whether postural coordination can be influenced during a visual interpersonal interaction. Based on previous research on postural coordination (Bardy et al., 1999; 2002) we know that in order to perform a suprapostural task, participants modify their postural coordination. They adapt the ankle-hip relative phase to the situation they are involved in. Consequently, we hypothesized that in interpersonal situations participants would adapt their own ankle-hip relative phase to be coordinated with their co-actor.

**Method**

Twenty participants stood in front of a target simulated on a monitor and were instructed to track the A-P oscillations of the target with an increase and a decrease of frequency ranging from 0.10 Hz to 0.75 Hz with step of 0.05 Hz (see Bardy et al. 2002 for more details). No instructions were given on the postural coordination they could adopt. They performed the tracking task in two conditions (Figure 1): paired (Duo condition) and alone (Solo condition).

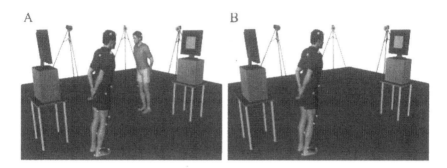

*Figure 1.* In the Duo condition (A) participants saw their co-actor in their peripheral view. In the Solo condition (B) participants were alone to perform the tracking task.

To analyze the influence of the interpersonal interaction on the spontaneous postural coordination dynamic, three variables were computed: 1) distribution and 2) standard deviation of the ankle-hip relative phase of each participant, indicating the coordination modes produced and their stability; 3) absolute difference between the postural transition frequencies (TF) of each paired participant in order to determine the influence of interpersonal interaction on the transition frequency.

**Results and Discussion**

1) The distribution of ankle-hip relative phase angles across nine phase regions was submitted to a 2 (Condition) × 9 (Phase Region) repeated measures ANOVA. Using the Greenhouse-Geisser correction, this analysis yielded a significant main effect of phase region ($F(8,152) = 63.26$, $p < .05$) and no significant interaction between phase region and condition ($F(8,152) = 0.20$, $p > .05$). These results showed that 1) anti-phase (and in-phase) coordination mostly emerged from this task and 2) there were no postural coordination differences in Duo and Solo conditions (Figure 2). Globally, participants did not produce more in-phase or anti-phase pattern during interpersonal interaction.

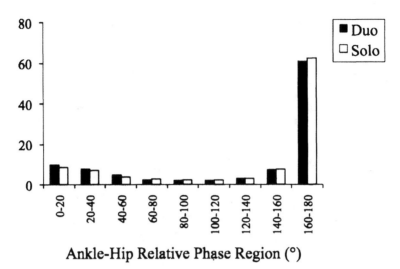

**Ankle-Hip Relative Phase Region (°)**

*Figure 2.* Distribution of ankle-hip relative phase angles for Duo (black) and Solo (white) conditions.

2) The standard deviation of ankle-hip relative phase was 8.24 (SD = 4.36) in Duo condition and 8.56 (SD = 5.44) in Solo condition. No difference in postural coordination stability was observed between Duo and Solo conditions. Interpersonal interaction did not affect the stability of postural coordination patterns produced by participants. This result suggests that the strength of the coupling of postural coordination is strong enough to not be influenced by the presence of the other participant. This is consistent with previous interpersonal coordination studies and indicates that intrapersonal coordination is more stable than visual interpersonal coordination (e.g., Schmidt et al., 1998).

3) The mean of the absolute difference between the transition frequencies (TF) was 0.19 Hz (SD = 0.14) for Duo condition and 0.24 Hz (SD = 0.14) for Solo condition. One factor ANOVA with repeated measures showed significant difference between these two conditions ($F_{(1,8)} = 10.78$ $p < .05$) (Figure 3 Top), revealing that when paired, participants spontaneously modified the frequency of their postural transition from one coordination mode to the other. Globally this result shows that during visual interaction, participants shifted postural coordination patterns either earlier or later than when alone, in order to adopt a similar postural pattern as the one performed by their co-actor (Figure 3 Bottom).

In conclusion, this study reveals that the exchange of visual information between two people can directly influence their postural coordination dynamic. This study can also be considered as a new paradigm in investigating postural coordination in a more social (and ecological) situation.

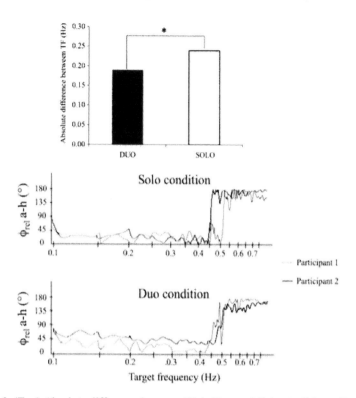

*Figure 3.* (Top) Absolute difference between TF in Duo and Solo conditions. (Bottom) Ankle-hip relative phase of two participants in Duo and Solo conditions illustrating that the presence of someone influenced participant's postural transition.

### References

Bardy, B.G., Marin, L., Stoffregen, T.A., & Bootsma, R.J. (1999). Postural coordination modes considered as emergent phenomena. *Journal of Experimental Psychology: Human Perception and Performance, 25*, 1284-1301.

Bardy, B.G., Oullier, O., Bootsma, R.J., & Stoffregen, T.A. (2002). Dynamics of human postural transitions. *Journal of Experimental Psychology: Human Perception and Performance, 28*, 499-514.

Schmidt, R.C., Bienvenu, M., Fitzpatrick, P.A., & Amazeen, P.G. (1998). A comparison of intra- and interpersonal coordination: Coordination breakdowns and coupling strength. *Journal of Experimental Psychology: Human Perception and Performance, 24*, 884-900.

Shockley, K., Santana, M.V., & Fowler, C.A. (2003). Mutual interpersonal postural constraints are involved in cooperative conversation. *Journal of Experimental Psychology: Human Perception and Performance, 29*, 326-332.

*Acknowledgements.* This research was supported by SKILLS, an Integrated Project (IST contract #035005) of the Commission of the European Community.

*Studies in Perception & Action X*
J. B. Wagman & C. C. Pagano (Eds.)
© 2009 Taylor & Francis Group, LLC

# Gaze Coordination between Car Drivers and Passengers: An Observation

Hiroshi Inou[1], Mamoru Sawada[1] & Hiroyuki Mishima[2]

[1]DENSO Corporation, Japan, [2]Waseda University, Japan

Passengers riding in a vehicle operated by an unskilled driver (e.g., a newly licensed driver) may feel fear or anxiety. One possible reason for such feelings is the rough operation and consequent rough movement of the vehicle. However, there seems to be an underlying perceptual cause as well. Consider the following two empirical facts: (1) an unskilled driver tends to focus their gaze on the near side of his/her front view while driving and (2) a passenger (riding in a vehicle with an unskilled driver), may be unconsciously induced to gaze at the near side of his/her front view relative to a distant landscape, although this is not the case when a skilled driver operates the vehicle. Why might this kind of gaze entrainment between a driver and a passenger occur? We propose that the structure of global optic flow presented to a passenger (or the passenger's visual system) is lawfully affected by a driver's "perceptual" skill (or the driver's gaze control, which could be considered as a reflection of his/her perceptual exploration) because the driver's operations that lawfully constrain the optic flow experienced in the vehicle must be controlled by the driver's perception. Therefore, when a driver's skill is poor, a passenger's gaze movement might be unstable, and he/she would feel uneasy. As the first step to addressing this gaze entrainment problem, we conducted an in-vehicle experiment.

**Method**

The experiment was conducted at a test track in the *DENSO* Abashiri Test Center (Hokkaido, Japan). The participants were: one skilled driver, who had been employed as a test driver at *DENSO* Corporation for 15 years, and one ordinary driver. In the "skilled driver condition," the skilled driver operated the test vehicle and the ordinary driver rode along in the passenger seat; in the "ordinary driver condition," the positions were reversed. The participants' gaze directions relative to the car's orientation were measured by recording their eye movements at 20 Hz with an eye tracking system (*NAC* Image Technology, EMR-8B). The movement data were smoothed using a Kalman filter. Two successive curves, "Corner A" (right-hand curve; radius = 100 m) and "Corner B" (left-hand curve; radius = 120 m), were defined as the experimental trials. Both the participants were asked to approach the first corner with an approximate velocity of 60 km/h while driving and look ahead when riding as the passenger.

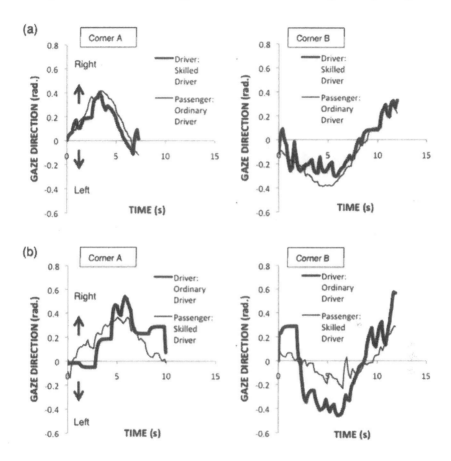

*Figure 1.* Gaze direction relative to the car's orientation as a function of time: (a) skilled driver condition; (b) unskilled driver condition

## Results and Discussion

The participants' gaze directions relative to the car's orientation in the skilled driver and ordinary driver conditions are shown in Figure 1. This figure illustrates the tendency for coordination between a driver's and passenger's gaze directions. Moreover, this coordination tendency appears to be stronger in the skilled driver condition than in the ordinary driver condition.

To examine the degree of gaze coordination between the driver and passenger, we used *cross-recurrence quantification analysis* (CRQA; Marwan, N., &

Kurths, 2002; Marwan, 2003; Shockley, 2005; Zbilut & Webber, 1992). In this analysis, the following CRQA parameter settings were used: embedding dimension = 6, delay = 0.25 s, radius = 0.15 radian, norm = Euclidean. The data used in the CRQA were not normalized.

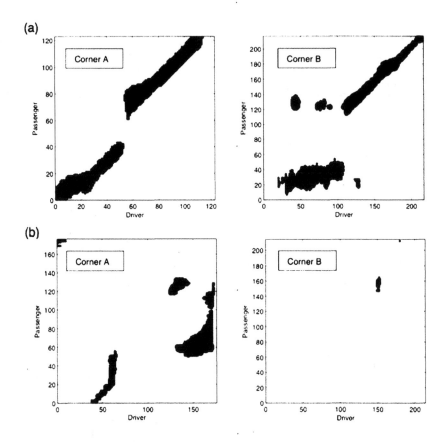

*Figure 2.* CRPs of the gaze directions of the driver and passenger in the ordinary driver condition: (a) skilled driver condition; (b) unskilled driver condition

The cross-recurrence plots (CRPs) for each data pair in each condition are shown in Figure 2. The *%recurrence* in each CRP is as follows: 0.104 and 0.08 for Corners A and B, respectively, in the skilled driver condition; 0.05 and 0.002 for Corners A and B, respectively, in the ordinary driver condition. These results support the strong coordination tendency in the skilled driver condition and the weak coordination tendency in the ordinary driver condition.

A driver's skill is directly reflected by the vehicle's behavior. Frequent changes in acceleration caused by poor operation of the vehicle by an unskilled driver produce disturbances in not only the driver's and passenger's bodies but also the optic flow field in front of the vehicle. On the other hand, the smooth and dexterous operations by a skilled driver will prevent such vibrations, maintain a dynamically stable optic flow, and guide the passenger's as well as the driver's gaze to an adequate point in the field of view. In future studies, we plan to explore the specific optic flow information that guides drivers' and passengers' gaze movements.

**References**

Marwan, N. (2003). *Encounters with neighbors: Current developments of concepts based on recurrence plots and their applications.* Doctoral thesis, University of Potsdam, Potsdam, Germany.

Marwan, N., & Kurths, J. (2002). Nonlinear analysis of bivariate data with cross recurrence plots. *Physics Letters A, 302*(5–6), 299–307.

Shockley, K. (2005). Cross recurrence quantification of interpersonal postural activity. In M. A. Riley & G. C. Van Orden (Eds.), *Tutorials in contemporary nonlinear methods for the behavioral sciences* (pp. 142–177). Retrieved October 13, 2006, from http://www.nsf.gov/sbe/bcs/pac/nmbs/nmbs.jsp

Zbilut, J. P., & Webber, C. L., Jr. (1992). Embeddings and delays as derived from quantification of recurrence plots. *Physics Letters A, 171*, 199–203.

*Studies in Perception & Action X*
J. B. Wagman & C. C. Pagano (Eds.)

# Target Distance Influences Interpersonal Postural Coordination

Alison Smith[1], Christie Pelzer[1], Russ Giveans[1], Kevin Shockley[2], & Thomas A. Stoffregen[1]

[1]University of Minnesota, [2]University of Cincinnati

When pairs of people converse while standing, their body sway exhibits spontaneous coordination (Shockley et al., 2003). When each member of a dyad converses with a different person, sway within the dyad is not coordinated, indicating that the effect is related to the interpersonal interaction. The strength of interpersonal coupling can be influenced by variations in the conversational interaction (Shockley et al., 2007). In addition, coordination might be influenced by characteristics of the targets of the conversation. For example, when dyads converse about something that they can see, postural coordination might be influenced by adjustments to posture to facilitate looking at objects of mutual interest.

Stoffregen et al. (1999) found that the magnitude of spontaneous body sway (in individuals) was related to the distance of visual targets: Sway was reduced when people fixated nearby targets, relative to sway during fixation of distant targets. This effect was functional in the sense that a given magnitude of sway would tend to have a more disruptive effect on fixation of nearby targets.

We evaluated whether distance-related effects of vision on stance in individuals might also affect the coordination of posture between members of a conversing dyad. To test this possibility, we replicated the task partner manipulation in the facing away condition from Shockley, et al. (2003), and added a manipulation of the distance of visual targets. We predicted that target distance would influence the sway of individuals in each dyad, and that target distance would influence the strength of interpersonal postural coordination.

### Method

Thirty students at the University of Minnesota participated in return for course credit. Participants were organized into 15 conversational pairs.

We used the picture puzzle task employed by Shockley et al. (2003), using the same cartoon pictures as that study. Within pairs, pictures were generally similar in appearance to one another with 10 subtle differences. In the Near condition, the cartoon pictures were 14.0 × 10.2 cm and were placed 0.5 m from the participants. In the Far condition, the same pictures were enlarged to 69.9 × 47.0 cm and were placed 2.5 m from the participants to achieve the same visual angle as the Near condition. Members of each dyad stood facing away from each other, on opposite sides of the emitter of a magnetic tracking system (Polhemus). Sensors were placed on the head (using an elastic headband) and hip (using tape) of each participant, and were sampled at 30 Hz. There were four trials per condition yielding 16 trials per participant pair. Participant pairs were asked to discuss their respective pictures to identify the 10 differences between the pictures. Participants either discussed their pictures with the other participant (Together) or with an experimental confederate (Confederate).

We used a 2 × 2 design, with Target Distance (Far vs. Near) and Conversational Partner (Together vs. Confederate), and four trials (per dyad) in each condition. Each trial was 120 s in duration. The two time series for a given pair for a given body location (head vs. hip) were submitted to a cross-recurrence analysis (see Shockley et al., 2003 for a more detailed discussion of this analysis). Mean %REC (the % of body configurations shared by a participant pair) and MAXLINE (the length of the longest consecutive sequence of recurring points for a given pair) for a given condition for a given body location for each participant pair were submitted to a 2 × 2 analysis of variance (ANOVA). Individual participants' positional data for head and hip body locations were also submitted to a 2 × 2 ANOVA.

### Results and Discussion

*Cross-recurrence analysis.* There were no significant effects in the MAXLINE variable. For the %RECUR variable the main effect of Partner was not significant for the head or the hips. Thus, we failed to replicate the effect of conversational partner on interpersonal postural coordination (Shockley et al., 2003, 2007), though as illustrated in Figure 1 the data showed the same trend as Shockley et al. (2003). However, for head motion the main effect of target distance on %RECUR was significant, $F(1, 14) = 5.35$, $p < .05$. As predicted, variations in the visual task (target distance) influenced the strength of interpersonal postural coupling. Participants showed less shared postural activity at the head for far targets as compared to near targets. The data for head motion are summarized in Figure 1.

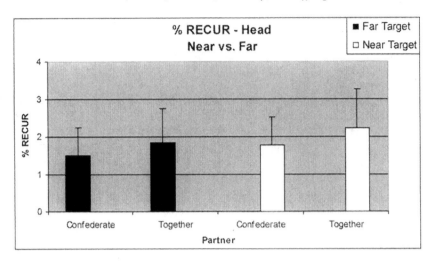

*Figure 1.* Results of cross-recurrence analysis, showing %RECUR for dyadic head movements as a function of conditions.

*Positional variability.* For the head, the mean variability of position in the ML axis was 1.30 cm in the Near condition, and 1.58 cm in the Far condition, $F(1, 29) = 14.737$, $p < .01$. For the hips, the ML means were 0.75 cm and 0.91 cm, respectively, $F(1,29) = 11.173$, $p < .01$. These effects replicate Stoffregen et al. (1999), and confirm our prediction. However, in the AP axis the influence of target distance on head movement was in the opposite direction (Mean$_{Near}$ = 2.02 cm, Mean$_{Far}$ = 1.77 cm), $F(1, 29) = 8.46$, $p < .01$.

We also found a significant effect of conversational partner on the positional variability of the head in the AP axis (Mean$_{Together}$ = 1.76 cm; Mean$_{Confederate}$ = 2.03 cm), $F(1, 29) = 5.47$, $p < .01$. A similar effect was observed by Stoffregen, Giveans, Villard, Yank, & Shockley (2009), and indicates that interpersonal influences on postural control are not limited to the dependent variables that emerge from cross-recurrence analysis.

Shockley et al. (2003) did not find a visual influence of the other participant on postural coordination. By contrast, in the present study we did find a visual influence of the target distance. Taken together, the results of our analysis of positional variability suggest that participants controlled AP body movement with respect to each other, and simultaneously controlled ML body movement with respect to the visual targets. Comparison of our two types of analysis (cross-recurrence and positional variability) suggest that the distance of visual targets influenced both the sway of individuals and the coupling of sway within dyads. One explanation for this pattern of results is that participants may have exhibited greater amplitude of eye movement in the Near condition as compared to the Far condition resulting in greater postural sway in the A-P direction (cf. Stoffregen, Bardy, Bonnet, & Pagulayan, 2006). This could be evaluated by tracking the eye movement patterns of participants in future studies.

**References**

Shockley, K., Baker, A. A., Richardson, M. J., & Fowler, C. A. (2007). Articulatory constraints on interpersonal postural coordination. *Journal of Experimental Psychology: Human Perception and Performance, 33,* 201-208.

Shockley, K., Santana, M. V., & Fowler, C. A. (2003). Mutual interpersonal postural constraints are involved in cooperative conversation. *Journal of Experimental Psychology: Human Perception and Performance, 29,* 326 – 332.

Stoffregen, T. A., Bardy, B. G., Bonnet, C. T., & Pagulayan, R. J. (2006). Postural stabilization of visually guided eye movements. *Ecological Psychology, 18,* 191-222.

Stoffregen, T. A., Giveans, M. R., Villard, S., Yank, J., Shockley, K. (2009). Interpersonal postural coordination on rigid and non-rigid surfaces. Ms. under review.

Stoffregen, T. A., Smart, L. J., Bardy, B. G., & Pagulayan, R. J. (1999). Postural stabilization of looking. *Journal of Experimental Psychology: Human Perception & Performance, 25,* 1641-1658.

*Studies in Perception & Action X*
J. B. Wagman & C. C. Pagano (Eds.)

# Chapter 3:

# Perception & Perceptual Learning

*Studies in Perception & Action X*
J. B. Wagman & C. C. Pagano (Eds.)
© 2009 Taylor & Francis Group, LLC

# Discrimination of Surfaces by Touching: Impact of Obstacles Attached to the Fingertip Upon Performance

Nobuhiro Furuyama[1], Hiroyuki Mishima[2], Shin Maruyama[1], & Masashi Takiyama[3]

[1] Research Organization of Information and Systems, National Institute of Informatics, [2]Waseda University, [3]The University of Tokyo, JAPAN

The present paper reports on an experiment that examined whether subjects can discriminate a piece of sandpaper of a certain roughness from that of another, by moving the tip of the right-hand index finger on the surfaces of the sandpapers with or without intermediate obstacles attached to the fingertip, and whether the movements systematically vary across different conditions. Their discrimination ability turned out not to be dramatically impeded, at least as far as the obstacles and the range of roughnesses of the sandpapers used in this experiment are concerned. However, the way the subjects examined sandpapers with the fingertip varied rather systematically, depending on what type of obstacles was attached to the fingertip.

## Method

The procedure of the experiment was as follows: Twenty-six healthy university undergraduate or graduate students and their friends participated in this study. They were in their twenties or thirties, all right handed with no physical problems with their hands. We recruited them from universities in Tokyo and compensated for their participation.

As for the stimuli, we used sandpaper, an abrasive material, of different surface roughnesses. To control the roughness of the sandpaper, we referred to the "grit number" system of the Japan Industrial Standards (JIS), which estimates the roughness by the size of abrasive particles on the sandpaper's surface. In this system, as in many others, the lower the number (e.g., #80) the rougher the sandpaper. We used sandpapers of #1000, #1500 and #2000 as the target stimuli for the subject to discriminate, and those of #80, #1200 and #5000 as obstacles attached to the fingertip.

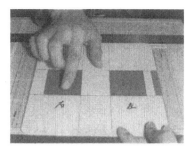

*Figure 1.* Experimental settings. Left: Subject touching the surface of a piece of sandpaper with the tip of the right-hand index finger. Right: Tip of the index finger wrapped with a piece of sandpaper. The finger was covered with a piece of scotch tape in the same way as with the sandpaper shown in this photo.

In each trial, two out of three different sandpapers were presented to the subject (Figure 1). The subject could not see the stimuli because of the curtain placed between the stimuli and the subject, but were allowed to touch them. The subject was asked to judge by touching with the tip of the right-hand index finger whether or not the two pieces of paper were the same in roughness, and, if not, which of the two was rougher than the other. The judgement had to be made within thirty seconds after each trial was started. They were additionally asked to rate their confidence about their judgement, using the 5 SD method. No feedback regarding the performance was given to the subject. During the entire experiment, the subjects were not allowed to see the sandpapers. They wore a pair of noise-cancelling headphones and listened to a commercially available audio file of the sound of rivers and/or waterfalls. This was meant to eliminate possible clues the subject might obtain from hearing the noises they made when they touched the sandpapers with their finger.

### Results and Discussion

*Performance:* Figure 2 shows the proportion of correct judgments by block of trials. The only difference among the subject groups (a, b, c) was the grit number of the sandpapers attached to the tip of the index finger in the third block. As shown in the figure there was no dramatic decrease in proportion of correct judgments as the subjects went through the blocks, suggesting that their ability discriminate was not impeded even when a piece of scotch tape or sandpaper was attached to their index finger.

*Confidence:* Figure 3 shows the average scores of the subject's confidence rating in the judgment. As we can see, the subjects rated their confidence lower when the fingertip was covered with obstacles than when it was not. Nonetheless, their performance did not necessarily become worse as they performed the experiment, and, quite interestingly, some subjects performed even better with the obstacles. It should also be noted that once the confidence rate dropped, it did not go up again even after an obstacle was taken away from the fingertip.

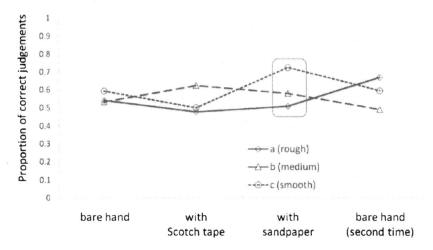

*Figure 2.* Proportion of correct judgments. The only difference among the groups was the grit number of the stimuli. Group a (rough: #80), Group b (medium: #1200), Group c (smooth: #5000) .

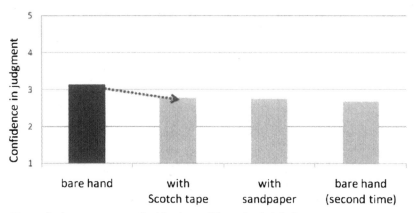

*Figure 3.* Average scores of subject's confidence in their judgment

*Patterns of touching behaviors:* We observed a number of variations in the touching behaviors. Figure 4 shows representative behaviours that were frequently and commonly used by the subjects. Additionally, when an obstacle was attached to the fingertip, the exploratory movements of the finger exhibited patterns different from the ones shown otherwise, but in rather predictable ways. For example, when the fingertip was covered with a piece of scotch tape, it moved much slower and over a much wider area on the surface of the sandpaper, and it pushed with higher pressure against the sandpaper than when it was not covered with anything. When the fingertip was covered with a piece of sandpaper, it moved much faster and over a narrower area, and it pushed against the surface more softly, i.e., with less pressure, than otherwise.

*Introspection:* During introspection, many of the subjects reported that they were not uncomfortable with the scotch tape or the sandpaper attached to their fingertip and that they consciously attempted to use new types of exploratory movements to obtain information to help them discriminate the target stimuli.

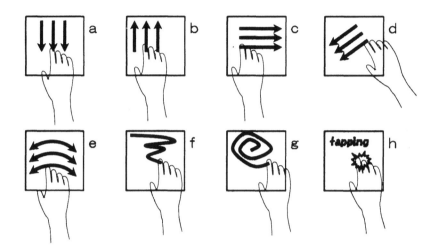

*Figure 4.* Pattern of touching behaviors. Movement speed and the way of combining patterns were variable. We frequently observed that patterns a, b, c, d and e were bi-directional.

These results suggest that people attempt different ways of touching objects to obtain the same information, despite differences in the interface between the object and the observer. This implies that the environment has a consistent and robust structure that can specify itself despite the differences and changes (at least to some extent) the observer might have to their perceptual system for detecting information. Our next goal would be to characterize the exploratory movement of the finger quantitatively as well as qualitatively, by measuring the trajectory, velocity, etc. of the movement, how strongly the finger pushes against the target stimulus, etc., and determine what is the invariant information at work here.

### References

David Katz (1925/1989). *The world of touch.* Erlbaum. Translation of *Der Aufbau der Tastwelt,* Leipzig: Barth.; edited and translated by Lester E. Krueger.

*Acknowledgements.* The first author of this study was supported by a National Institute of Informatics internal research grant from 2007 through 2008.

*Studies in Perception & Action X*
J. B. Wagman & C. C. Pagano (Eds.)
© 2009 Taylor & Francis Group, LLC

# Integration of Visuo-Haptic Information for Judging Object Size

Chia-Hao Lu, Joshua Aman, & Jüergen Konczak

Human Sensorimotor Control Laboratory,
School of Kinesiology, University of Minnesota, Minneapolis, MN, U.S.A.

Humans routinely rely on visual and haptic information for recognizing and manipulating objects in the environment. In trying to understand how haptic and visual information are integrated, researchers have elucidated the relative contribution of visual and haptic sense by introducing visual-haptic discrepancies experimentally.

Previous studies on judging vertical object size showed that the visuo-haptic integration occurs in a statistically optimal fashion by following a maximum likelihood function (Ernst & Banks, 2002; Gori, Del Viva, Sandini & Burr, 2008; Helbig & Ernst, 2008). Their findings also indicated that integrating redundant visual and haptic information of the same object improves the accuracy of the size estimate when comparing the size of two objects. However, these studies did not address the issue of how the order of presenting visual or haptic information influences the sensitivity of size perception when asked to discriminate between two objects.

In this psychophysical study, we determined the just noticeable difference thresholds for vertical size judgment. In a first set of experiments the thresholds were determined on the basis that only one modality was available (vision only or haptic only). In a second set of experiments the stimulus presentation order (visual or haptic or simultaneous) was altered to determine the relative contribution of each sense for size perception as a function of when the information became available.

### Methods

Healthy college level students (aged 19 – 25 yrs, n=10) recruited from the University of Minnesota participated in the experiment on a voluntary basis. The participants were all right handed. There were four different conditions that were separately presented to participants. In each condition, participants were presented with a reference block (6 cm tall) and a randomly chosen comparison block (heights were between 5.2 cm and 6.8 cm tall). Widths of the blocks were all equal (9 cm).

The participants were seated on a height-adjustable chair in front of the experimental apparatus with their hand resting on a visible start location. The experimental apparatus was made of a rectangle wood board, which acts as a blind, with one block in the front and one block behind the blind. Participant's viewing distance from the front (visual) block was 30 cm. Participants used only their right hand to haptically explore the block behind the blind, using only their thumb and index finger.

Participants were asked which of the two blocks was taller and were instructed to make verbal size judgments in the four following conditions: (1) Vision only; participants only viewed the reference and comparison blocks before making a size judgment. (2) Haptic only; vision was blocked. Participants haptically explored the reference block first, followed by exploring a comparison block. (3) Visual-to-Haptic (V-H); participants first explored the reference block visually and then haptically explored the comparison block. (4) Haptic-to-Visual (H-V); participants first explored the reference block haptically and were then presented with the visual comparison block and subsequently indicated which block was taller. The reference blocks and comparison blocks were randomly presented for some trials to reduce an order effect. The viewing or haptic exploration time was set to 4 seconds and was held constant in all conditions. Each comparison was repeated three times in each condition.

**Results and Discussion**

Four sigmoidal sensitivity functions were created based on each condition. For each sensitivity function, a just noticeable difference threshold at 75% correct response level was computed. In addition, we determined the region of uncertainty, defined as the region between the 25% - 75% correct response level (i.e., the region where object size was not accurately judged). The main results are:

**1**) Vision was more sensitive than haptics for object size discrimination when only one modality was present (region of uncertainty for *vision-only*: 5.86 - 6.06 cm; *haptic-only*: 5.88 - 6.28 cm; see Fig. 1a, 1b). The region of uncertainty was larger in the *haptic-only* condition (*vision-only*: 0.2cm; *haptic-only*: 0.4cm).

**2**) When information from both senses was present, the regions of uncertainty increased with respect to both vision-only and haptic-only conditions (*V-H*: 0.52 cm ; *H-V*: 0.47 cm, see Figure 1).

**3**) For cross-modality comparison conditions, the region of uncertainty was smaller in *H-V* condition than in the *V-H*.

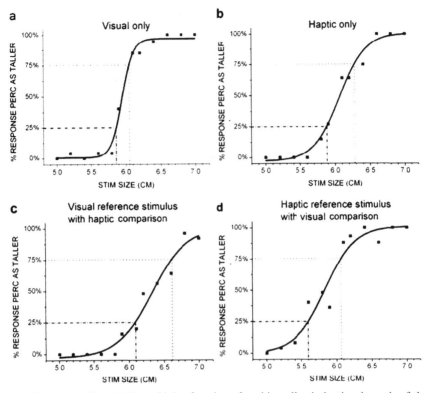

*Figure 1*. Sigmoidal sensitivity functions for object discrimination in each of the four conditions.

Our data confirm previous findings about the saliency of vision for size perception. However, we found that the order in which object size information becomes available may be important. Allowing for haptic exploration before viewing increased discrimination sensitivity. Interestingly, participants tended to underestimate size in the *H-V* condition, while overestimating size in the *V-H* condition. This indicates that the visuo-haptic integration process for discriminating object size is affected by what type of sensory information becomes available first (i.e., direction of the sensitivity function shifts accordingly). In order to further clarify the relative contribution of each sense for object size discrimination, we are currently investigating size perception acuity during the simultaneous presentation of haptic and visual cues. It is plausible that the weighting of visual and haptic information for object size perception changes as the presentation order changes.

The data of the vision-only condition and haptic-only condition replicated findings indicating that vision is more sensitive for size discrimination (Ernst & Banks, 2002; Gori, Del Viva, Sandini & Burr, 2008; Helbig & Ernst, 2008). However, while the 75% thresholds were different between vision-only and haptic-only conditions, the lower boundary of the regions of uncertainty (25% correct response level) were approximately the same for both vision-only and haptic-only conditions. This indicates that it is more difficult to determine differences haptically only when the comparison blocks were larger than the reference block.

There are two possible explanations to why discrimination thresholds were different in *V-H* versus the *H-V* condition. One explanation, as stated above, is that the sensitivity of object size discrimination is influenced by how the first object was perceived (visually or haptically). An alternative explanation for our data may indicate that judgements during the H-V and V-H may be influenced by the distance the blocks were away from the eyes and the body. In our setup, the physical distance of the visually perceived block was closer than the haptically explored block. That is, the egocentric distances for perceiving the objects were different for each modality. It could be possible that this arrangement introduced a bias which led to the discrepancy in threshold levels between *H-V* and *V-H* conditions. A final point of interest is that in the *V-H* condition, the lower boundary of the region of uncertainty was 6.1 cm, which means that in 75% of the responses, participants incorrectly determined the 6.1 cm block to be smaller than the standard 6.0 cm block, while 100% of the participants correctly determined the 5.9 cm block to be smaller than the 6.0 cm standard block, both being 1 cm difference in height when compared to the standard block. A new apparatus is currently being used to control for egocentric distances.

This study was designed to provide baseline data for evaluating clinical populations with proprioceptive or tactile deficits such as patients with Parkinson's disease or dystonia. In addition, future studies might explore how the task requirements (perceptual judgment vs. object-based action) would affect the weighting of haptic & visual information during the sensory integration process.

### References

Ernst, M. O., & Banks, M. S. (2002). Humans integrate visual and haptic information in a statistically optimal fashion. *Nature, 415*(6870), 429-433.

Gori, M., Del Viva, M., Sandini, G., & Burr, D. C. (2008). Young children do not integrate visual and haptic form information. *Current Biology : CB, 18*(9), 694-698.

Helbig, H. B., & Ernst, M. O. (2008). Visual-haptic cue weighting is independent of modality-specific attention. *Journal of Vision, 8*(1), 21.1-21.16.

*Studies in Perception & Action X*
J. B. Wagman & C. C. Pagano (Eds.)
© 2009 Taylor & Francis Group, LLC

# Perceiving by Dynamic Touch
# with and without Hands

Zsolt Palatinus[1], Claudia Carello[1], & Michael T. Turvey[1,2]

[1]Center for the Ecological Study of Perception and Action, University of Connecticut, USA, [2] Haskins Laboratories, New Haven, CT, USA.

Non-visual perception of a wielded object's properties is based on the moments of the object's mass distribution. The three moments (mass, static moment and moment of inertia) are invariant over variations in the forces brought to bear on an object and on the body's tissues during wielding. Previous research has shown that perception by dynamic touch is not sensation-based (Carello, 1992), not anatomically specific (Hajnal et al., 2007a), and not dependent on specific kinematics (Pagano et al., 1993). Importantly, however, it can be selective (Turvey et al., 1996; Cooper et al., 2000).

In the present research we extended these investigations beyond the limbs. The particulars of morphology and physiology—even though they may be linked to traditional measures of local sensory acuity—should not matter to the capacity of connective tissue to be structured lawfully and globally in support of dynamic touch (Carello, Silva, Kinsella-Shaw, & Turvey, 2009). However wielding is accomplished, a deformation field is induced that is lawfully related to properties of the wielded object. The reported experiments test and compare the capabilities of the hand and the torso, anatomical links with very different roles in manipulating objects. Experiment 1 was designed to establish the basic perceptual capability of the torso, given that it is typically construed more as a support link than as an effector. Experiment 2 compared torso and hand directly.

## Method

For wielding by torso, rods were attached   at their middle to the upper back with a harness (Figure 1, left). For wielding by hand, rods were grasped in the middle. Perceivers (8 per group) used a magnitude production pulley to report either whole length (markers were moved to indicate both ends of the rod) or partial length (a single marker was moved to indicate the length of the rod from the attachment point to the left end).  Both experiments used three rod lengths and three mass conditions. Rods in Experiment 1 were larger ($L$ = 72, 96, and 120 cm; diameter = 2.54 cm; attached mass = 150 g) than rods in Experiment 2 ($L$ = 45, 60 and 75 cm; diameter = 1.25 cm; attached mass = 50 g). The attached mass was affixed at $1/8\ L$ (the rod could be oriented to place the mass on the left or the right) or the rod remained plain (Figure 1, middle).

In Experiment 1, participants received four repetitions of each $L \times M$ combination resulting in 36 trials, randomized within blocks. In Experiment 2, they received three repetitions of the $L \times M$ combinations, randomized within effector block resulting in 54 total trials.

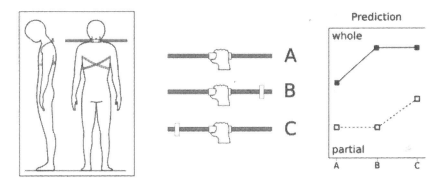

*Figure 1.* The style of the attachment (left), the three mass positions (middle), and the predicted pattern of the judgments (right).

### Results and Discussion

*Perceived Length, $L_{033P}$.* A 2 (attention: whole vs. partial length) × 3 (rod length) × 3 (attached mass position) between-participants ANOVA on $L_P$ 3 in Experiment 1 revealed main effects of attention, $F(1, 17) = 16.9$, $p < .001$, attached mass position, $F(2, 17) = 18.6$, $p < .001$, and a Mass 33 × Attention interaction, $F(2, 17) = 57.3$, $p < .001$. Selective perception by the torso was achieved in the predicted pattern (Figure 2a).

A 2 (attention) × 2 (effector) × 3 (rod length) × 3 (attached mass position) between-participant ANOVA on $L_P$ in Experiment 2 revealed main effects of attention, $F(1, 35) = 21.8$, $p < .001$, mass position, $F(2, 35) = 30.5$, $p < .001$, and a Mass × Attention interaction, $F(2, 35) = 94.7$, $p < .001$. Neither effector, $F(1, 35) = 2.42$, $p = .124$, nor its interactions (*8 Fs $\approx$ 1*) were significant. The predicted pattern was obtained for both effectors (see Figure 2b).

*Reliability and Accuracy.* Reliability of length judgments was assessed by taking the average deviation of an individual's responses as a % of that person's mean $L_P$. A measure of accuracy was provided by mean root square (MRS) error, deviation of an individual's responses as a % of actual extent (for details, see Hajnal et al. 2007a,b). In Experiment 1, a 2 (attention) × 2 (analysis: reliability vs. MRS) between participant ANOVA on these measures revealed a main effect of analysis, $F(1, 12) = 34.2$, $p < .001$. MRS is greater than reliability, indicating a systematic influence on $L_P$ beyond actual length (and apart from random variation). This is the usual finding and is related to the importance of inertial constraints (see below). There was no interaction between analysis and attention, < 1. MRS averaged 38.6%, reliability averaged 14.2%.

In Experiment 2, a 2 (attention) × 2 (grip) × 2 (reliability vs. MRS) between-participant ANOVA again revealed a main effect of analysis, $F(2, 35) = 20.2$, $p < .002$. Neither the effect of grip nor its interaction with analysis was significant, both $Fs < 1$. MRS averaged 40.6% for judgments by hand and 41.8% for judgments by torso. Reliability averaged 10.6% for judgments by hand and 10.3% for judgments by torso.

*Inertial scaling.* At the outset, we noted that non-visual perception of a wielded object's properties is based on the moments of the object's mass distribution. The difference between MRS and reliability highlights this dependence: Perceived length is constrained by something other than actual length. Following common practice (e.g., Cooper et al., 2000), we conducted regressions of log perceived length on log $I_{xx}$ for both experiments. The regression analysis for perceived whole length revealed a significant dependence on $I_{xx}$ for both torso and hand, with virtually all of the variance accounted for ($r^2 = .97$). For perceived partial length, a further regression of residuals on $I_{yz}$ was significant for both torso and hand ($r^2 = .92$).

The present results build on findings that the foot is comparable to the hand in the perception of object length by dynamic touch even in selective tasks (Hajnal et al., 2007b). These capabilities are not restricted to the limbs. Tissue deformation throughout the muscular-skeletal system allows mechanoreceptors to extract the invariant specific to object extent. More generally, perceivers seemingly assemble the haptic system into a smart subsystem to pick up the moments specific to a particular property. It has been suggested, that this function may arise from a synergy of the mechanoreceptors and the attendant neural and fascia nets (Turvey & Fonseca, 2009). Our findings support the hypothesis that in detecting invariants, the haptic substrate behaves in a field-like fashion suggestive of a tensegrity structure—interconnected tension-supporting components and isolated compression-bearing components that distribute stresses to ensure force balance and shape stabilization.

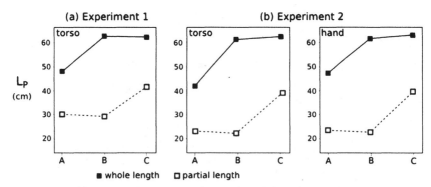

*Figure 2.* The expected data pattern for mass conditions A, B, and C was obtained in both experiments.

**References**

Carello, C., Fitzpatrick, P., Domaniewicz, I., Chan, T.-C., Turvey, M.T. (1992) Effortful touch with minimal movement. *Journal of Experimental Psychology: Human Perception and Performance, 18,* 290–302.

Carello, C., Silva, P. L., Kinsella-Shaw, J. M., & Turvey, M. T. (2009). Sensory and motor challenges to muscle-based perception. *Brazilian Journal of Physical Therapy, 12,* 339-350.

Cooper, M., Carello, C., & Turvey, M. T. (2000). Perceptual independence of whole length, partial length, and hand position in wielding a rod. *Journal of Experimental Psychology: Human Perception and Performance, 26,* 74-85.

Hajnal, A., Fonseca, S. T., Harrison, S., Kinsella-Shaw, J. M., & Carello, C. (2007a). Comparison of dynamic (effortful) touch by hand and foot. *Journal of Motor Behavior, 39,* 82-88.

Hajnal, A., Fonseca, S., Kinsella-Shaw, J., Silva, P., Carello, C., & Turvey, M. T. (2007b). Haptic selective attention by foot and by hand. *Neuroscience Letters, 419,* 5-9.

Pagano, C. C., Fitzpatrick, P., & Turvey, M. T. (1993). Tensorial basis to the constancy of perceived extent over variations of dynamic touch. *Perception & Psychophysics, 54,* 43-54.

Runeson, S. (1977). On the possibility of "smart" perceptual mechanisms. *Scandinavian Journal of Psychology, 18,* 172-179.

Turvey, M. T., & Fonseca, S. (2009). Nature of motor control: Perspectives and issues. In D. Sternad (Ed.) *Progress in motor control: A multidisciplinary perspective* (pp. 93-123). New York: Springer Verlag.

van de Langenberg, R., Kingma, I. and Beek, P. J. (2006). Mechanical invariants are implicated in dynamic touch as a function of their salience in the stimulus flow. *Journal of Experimental Psychology: Human Perception and Performance, 32,* 1093–1106.

*Acknowledgments.* This research was supported by NSF Grant SBR 00-04097 and a grant from the Provost's Office at the University of Connecticut.

*Studies in Perception & Action X*
J. B. Wagman & C. C. Pagano (Eds.)
© 2009 Taylor & Francis Group, LLC

# Apparent Point of Rotation Manipulation Affects Multimodal Heaviness Perception

Laura Bachus, Kevin Shockley, & Michael A. Riley

University of Cincinnati, Cincinnati, OH USA

Heaviness perception is one of the oldest problems in perceptual psychology (Charpentier, 1891) and yet a unified theory to explain this phenomenon remains conspicuously absent. Non-visual heaviness perception (i.e., perception of heaviness via touching/hefting an object) has largely been accounted for in terms of rotational inertia—the resistance of a wielded object to applied wielding torque (e.g., Amazeen & Turvey, 1996; Shockley, Grocki, Carello, & Turvey, 2001). Inertia for rotation in the sagittal plane can be defined as:

$$I \approx mass \cdot d^2 \qquad (1)$$

where $d$ is the distance between the center of mass *(CM)* and the point of rotation (i.e. the wrist). Thus, an object's inertia can be manipulated by either changing the mass or the distribution of that mass around the point of rotation. For example, increasing the distance of a mass on a wielded object away from the wrist makes the object feel heavier (Amazeen & Turvey, 1996). A similar change in inertia can be achieved by changing the object's point of rotation. When an object is held closer to its center, it will offer less resistance to a given applied torque than when held at one of its ends.

Heaviness perception is also influenced by vision, however. For example, as objects become larger, they are typically perceived as lighter, even when controlling for rotational inertia (Amazeen, 1997). However, theoretical accounts of size do not explain why size influences appear to depend on seeing the wielded objects in motion (Masin & Crestoni, 1981). Streit and colleagues have made efforts to understand the role of vision in heaviness perception based on our understanding of rotational inertia. They evaluated the influence of changing an object's *apparent* motion in response to applied wielding torque based on the equation:

$$N = I\omega \qquad (2)$$

where $I$ is rotational inertia, $\dot{\omega}$ is rotational acceleration and $N$ is applied torque. They hypothesized that rotational inertia is specified multimodally by the following relation:

$$I_{specified} = \frac{N}{\omega_{apparent}},$$ (3)

where $\dot{\omega}_{apparent}$ is the apparent rotational acceleration—the acceleration of a virtual object moving in real time with the actual wielded object (see Figure 1) to which a scaling factor (rotational gain) is applied to manipulate apparent responsiveness of the wielded object to applied torques. Thus, just as an object that is highly responsive to an applied torque (i.e., low inertia) is perceived as light, an object that *appears* to be highly responsive specifies to a perceiver that the object has low inertia and the object is perceived as light (Streit et al., 2007).

At issue is whether the Streit et al. (2007) multimodal inertia model can account for other visual influences (e.g., object size). One possibility is that the apparent distribution of mass about a point of rotation may influence heaviness perception in a similar fashion to actual changes in rotational inertia described above. For example, if $d$ in Equation 1 is replaced with $d_{apparent}$—the apparent distance of the center of mass from the point of rotation for a virtual object— then rotational inertia is likewise specified multimodally by the following relation:

$$I_{specified} = mass \cdot d_{apparent}^{2}.$$ (4)

Linking Equations 3 and 4 yields

$$mass \cdot d_{apparent}^{2} = \frac{N}{\omega_{apparent}},$$ (5)

which offers a candidate perceptual variable that would capture influences of both apparent rotational motion and changes in the apparent mass distribution that would accompany size changes (Amazeen & Turvey, 1996)—multimodally specified mass:

$$mass_{specified} = \frac{N}{\omega_{apparent} \cdot d_{apparent}^{2}}$$ (6)

We evaluated a novel prediction from Equation 6. If multimodal heaviness perception is sensitive to mass$_{specified}$, then decreasing the apparent distance of the center of mass from the point of rotation ($d_{apparent}$) should increase the perceived heaviness of the object.

**Method**

In Experiment 1 (n=20), participants wielded objects while viewing the corresponding motion of virtual objects in a visual display and reported how heavy the objects felt (see Figure 1). Motion sensors on the base of the object handles tracked the movement of the objects. A computer projected virtual counterparts of the wielded objects onto a screen in view of the participants. For each trial, participants wielded the two objects back and forth between two virtual targets and rated one (test object) relative to the other (standard; heaviness=100). The test object was projected in four different apparent point-of-rotation (i.e., $d_{apparent}$) configurations and two different values of rotational gain (0.8 and 1.2 × actual rotation). The latter manipulation was included to encourage a variety of responses in case the $d_{apparent}$ manipulation did not influence heaviness. Each configuration was repeated four times in blocks of eight trials for a total of 32 trials, with trials randomized within each block for each participant. The objects' motion was recorded during each trial and used to generate identical visual displays for Experiment 2.

During the vision-only condition of Experiment 2 (n=20), participants watched the motion recorded from Experiment 1 (without wielding them) and were asked to report how heavy the test object looked. During the wielding-only condition, participants were also asked to provide non-visual heaviness judgments for the wielded object.

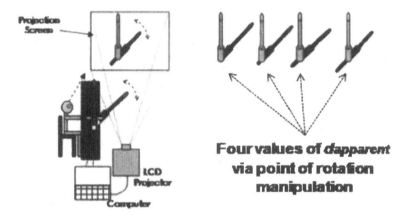

*Figure 1.* Illustration of the virtual reality paradigm (left) and the $d_{apparent}$ manipulation (right).

**Results and Discussion**

Participants' mean heaviness reports were submitted to a 2 (rotational gain) × 4 ($d_{apparent}$) repeated measures analysis of variance. In Experiment 1 perceived heaviness was inversely proportional to rotational gain, $F(1,19) = 25.52$, $p <$ .0001 and perceived heaviness was inversely proportional to $d_{apparent}$, $F(3, 19) = 12.92$, $p < .0001$), with no interaction. In Experiment 2 there were no significant effects ($Fs < 1$).

The results supported our hypothesis and demonstrated a novel visual influence on heaviness perception. As the apparent distance between the center of mass and the point of rotation increases, perceived heaviness decreases. Perceptual sensitivity to the hypothesized quantity $mass_{specified}$ may, therefore, account for previously observed visual influences of both rotational acceleration (e.g., Streit et al., 2007) and size (e.g., Ellis & Lederman, 1998) on heaviness perception under a common theoretical framework based on rotational inertia. For example, when objects increase in length, the center of mass extends farther from the point of rotation and yields a decrease in perceived heaviness. However, influences of apparent size and rotational gain only occurred during multimodal (e.g. visual + haptic) perception, suggesting that these factors only influence heaviness perception by virtue of their relation to applied wielding torques.

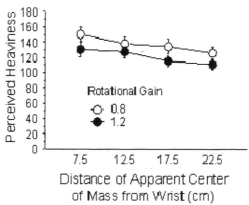

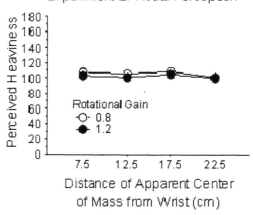

*Figure 2.* Results of Experiments 1 and 2.

## References

Amazeen, E. (1997). The effects of volume on perceived heaviness by dynamic touch: With and without vision. *Ecological Psychology, 9,* 245-263.

Amazeen, E., & Turvey, M.T. (1996). Weight perception and the haptic size-weight illusion are functions of the inertia tensor. *Journal of Experimental Psychology: Human Perception and Performance, 22,* 213-232.

Chapentier, A. (1891). Analyse expérimentale de quelques éléments de la sensation de poids [Experimental study of some aspects of weight perception]. *Archives de Physiologie Normales et Pathologiques, 13,* 122-135.

Ellis, R. R. & Lederman, S. J. (1998). The golf-ball illusion: evidence for top-down processing in weight perception. *Perception, 27,* 193-201.

Garg, A., & Saxena, U. (1980). Container characteristics and maximum acceptable weight of lift. *Human Factors, 22,* 487-495.

Masin, C. S. & Crestoni, L. (1981). Experimental demonstration of the sensory basis of the size-weight illusion. *Perception & Psychophysics, 44,* 309-312.

Streit, M., Shockley, K., & Riley, M. (2007). Rotational inertia and multimodal heaviness perception. *Psychonomic Bulletin & Review, 14,* 1001-1006.

*Acknowledgements.* This research was supported by NSF grant #0716319.

*Studies in Perception & Action X*
J. B. Wagman & C. C. Pagano (Eds.)
© 2009 Taylor & Francis Group, LLC

# Twelve-Month-Olds' Discrimination of Monkey Faces: Evidence for Perceptual Narrowing?

Ross Flom, Melissa Wright, Amanda Phillippi, Tom Beckstead, Jacob Jones, Harrison Allen, & Danny Boysen

Department of Psychology
Brigham Young University

It is well known from birth that faces are salient, preferred over other stimuli (Easterbrook, Kisilevsky, Hains & Muir, 1999; Barrera & Mauer, 1981), and are readily discriminated (Mauer & Young, 1983; Pascalis & de Schonen, 1994). It has also been shown that over the course of development infants' proclivity for face discrimination is influenced by their social environment. Pascalis, de Hann, and Nelson (2002), for example, demonstrate that 6-month-olds are able to discriminate various monkey faces as well as human faces whereas 9-month-olds can only discriminate different human faces. Importantly, however, if 6-month-olds receive 1-2 minutes per day of familiarization with photographs of monkey faces three months later the now 9-month-olds can still discriminate unfamiliar and familiar monkey faces (Pascalis, Scott, Kelly, Shannon, Nicholson, Coleman, & Nelson, 2005).

Like face perception, infants' discrimination of speech also varies as a function of experience and exposure. Specifically, 4- to 6-month-olds discriminate speech sounds in their native and non-native languages; however, by 10- to 12-months of age infants can only discriminate speech sounds common to their native language (Kuhl, Williams, Lacerda, Stevens, & Lindblom, 1992; Werker & Tees, 1984). More recently, however, Kuhl, Tsao, and Liu (2003) have shown that providing 9-month-olds with exposure to non-native phonemes extends their discrimination of these phonemes to 12-months of age.

The fact that within the first months of life infants' discriminate a variety of faces and speech sounds and by infants first birthday this ability has "narrowed" to reflect infants' perceptual experience has become known as "perceptual narrowing" (Pascalis, et al., 2002). Critical, however, is the assumption that perceptual narrowing reflects a relatively permanent change in perceptual abilities as well as a change in early neural architecture (Scott, Pascalis, & Nelson, 2008). The purpose of this experiment is to examine whether infants' ability to discriminate unfamiliar monkey faces truly narrows. One possibility, and the possibility examined in this experiment, is that 12-month-olds who have never been previously exposed to monkey faces, can discriminate unfamiliar monkey faces when they are provided longer periods of familiarization and longer times to visually compare the two faces. In this experiment, we examined 12-month-olds' discrimination of monkey faces when provided 40s or 20s of familiarization and were subsequently allowed to compare the two faces for 10s or 5s.

## Method

Forty-eight 12-month-olds were familiarized to a static color display of a Barbary Macaque (*Macaca sylvanus*). The faces used by Pascalis et. al. (2002) were used in the current experiment. Figure 1 provides an example of the stimuli. Infants were randomly assigned to one of two familiarization conditions (40s or 20s). During familiarization infants saw the same face side-by-side on two video monitors. Following familiarization infants received two test trials where the face of familiarization was presented on one video monitor and a novel face was presented on the adjacent monitor. For those infants who received 40s of familiarization each of the two visual-paired comparison test trial were 10s in length. Those infants who received 20s of familiarization each test trials was 5s in length. The lateral position of the novel face was alternated between the two test trials. Following the two test trials the procedure was repeated where each infant received a different pair of faces.

*Figure 1:* Examples of stimuli: Each infant received two pairs.

**Results and Discussion**

The primary dependent variable was infants' proportion of total looking time (PTLT) directed toward the novel face. Proportions were derived by dividing the time infants spent looking to the novel face by the time spent looking at both faces. An overall PTLT was derived by averaging across the four test trials. Infants' proportion of total looking time (PTLT) to the novel face is presented in Figure 2. Following 20s of familiarization and the two 5s visual-paired comparison test trials 12-month-olds failed to show a reliable preference for the novel or familiar face $M$ = 49%; $t$ (23) = .98, $p$ > .1 Within the 20s familiarization condition 12-month-olds' looking behavior between the first familiarization and test-trial pairing and the second pairing did not significantly differ ($p$>.1). Following 40s of familiarization and two 10s test trials 12-month-olds, however, showed reliable discrimination of the novel and familiar monkey face, $M$ = 54%; $t$ (23) = 3.1, $p$ = .015. In addition, 12-month-olds showed reliable discrimination for the first pair, $M$ = 55%; $t$ (23) = 2.8, $p$ = .02, as well as the second, $M$ = 53%; $t$ (23) = 2.6, $p$ = .02. Finally, infants looking to the novel face was significantly longer in the 40s familiarization condition compared to the 20s condition $t$ (23) = 4.1, $p$ < .01. Thus 12-month-olds show reliable discrimination of previously unfamiliar monkey faces when provided longer familiarization and increased time to visually compare the two faces.

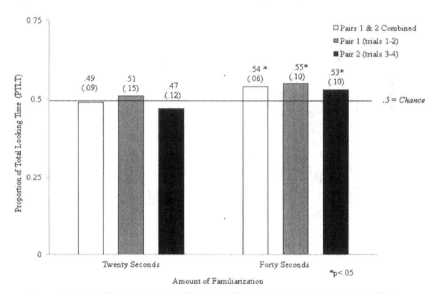

*Figure 2:* Mean (SD) proportion of total looking time (PTLT) to the novel face.

These results demonstrate that infants' ability to discriminate unfamiliar monkey faces is not "lost" or "perceptually narrowed" during the course of development. Specifically, our results demonstrate that 12-month-olds who have limited exposure and time to compare the two faces do not show significant evidence of discriminating the novel and familiar face. However, those infants who received longer periods of familiarization and comparison reliably discriminated the faces. Finally, it is somewhat ironic that studies of perceptual narrowing have been used to highlight the experience dependent nature of perceptual learning where the current results, that do not show a perceptual decline, also highlight the experience dependent nature of perceptual learning.

## References

Barrera, M., & Maurer, D. (1981). Recognition of mother's photographed face by the three month old infant. *Child Development, 52,* 714-716.

Easterbrook, M., Kisilevsky, B., Hains, S., & Muir, D. (1999). Faceness or complexity: evidence from newborn visual tracking of facelike stimuli. *Infant Behavior and Development, 22,* 17-35.

Kuhl, P. K., Tsao. F.-M., & Liu, H.-M. (2003). Foreign-language experience in infancy: Effects of short-term exposure and social interaction on phonetic learning. *Proceedings of the National Academy of Sciences, USA, 100,* 9096-9101.

Kuhl, P. K., Williams, K. A., Lacerda, F., Stevens, K. N., & Lindblom, B. (1992). Linguistic experience alters phonetic perception in infants by 6 months of age. *Science, 255,* 606-608.

Maurer, D., & Young, R.E. (1983). Newborns' following of natural and distorted arrangements of facial features. *Infant Behavior and Development, 6,* 127-131.

Pascalis, O., de Hann, M., & Nelson, C.A. (2002). Is face processing species-specific during the first year of life? *Science, 296,* 1321-1323

Pascalis, O., & de Schonen, S. (1994). Recognition in 3- to 4-day-old human neonates. *NeuroReport, 5,* 1721-1724.

Pascalis, O., Scott, L.S., Kelly, D. J., Shannon, R.W., Nicholson, E., Coleman, M., & Nelson, C.A. (2005). Plasticity of face processing in infancy. *Proceedings of the National Academy of Sciences, USA, 102,* 5297-5300.

Scott, L.S., Pascalis, O., & Nelson, C.A. (2007) A domain general theory of the development of perceptual discrimination. *Current Directions in Psychological Science, 16(4),* 197-201

Werker, J. F., & Tees, R.C. (1984). Cross-language speech perception: Evidence for perceptual reorganization during the first year of life. *Infant Behavior and Development, 7,* 49-63.

*Studies in Perception & Action X*
J. B. Wagman & C. C. Pagano (Eds.)
© 2009 Taylor & Francis Group, LLC

# Human Sensitivity to Local Taus

## Nam-Gyoon Kim[1] & Keonho Shin[2]

[1]Department of Psychology, Keimyung University, Daegu, Korea
[2]Department of Education, Kangnam University, Yongin, Korea

When an object moves directly toward an observer, its arrival time can be predicted from two types of local perturbation in the optic flow. The visual angle subtended by any two texture elements on the surface of the object expands as it approaches the observer, as does the image corresponding to the entire contour of the object. The inverse of the relative rates of each of these two types of expansion defines the time to contact (TTC). Tresilian (1991) refers to these two optical quantities as local tau1 (one-dimensional property) and local tau2 (two-dimensional property), respectively.

For these quantities to be available, the contour of the object must remain constant over the course of its approach. If the object is non-spherical, such as a rugby ball or an American football, that rotates on its way to the receiver, not only does its shape deform irregularly, but the surface texture elements move about, sometimes even disappearing from view. How might the visual system cope under such circumstances?

Gray and Regan (2000) studied the estimation of TTC for a rotating non-spherical object. In that study, an oval object rotated about its horizontal axis over the simulated path of approach so that the distance between the two end points along the vertical axis of the object changed, altering the outline of the object from ellipse to circle or circle to ellipse. Local tau 2, therefore, failed to convey veridical TTC information. However, the distance between the two end points along the horizontal axis remained constant, which could have been used to extract local tau1. Gray and Regan observed that TTC estimation was unreliable under monocular viewing, but improved under binocular viewing.

Are human observers incapable of estimating TTC of a tumbling rugby ball while watching it with a single eye, as Gray and Regan (2000) contend? Everyday experiences suggest otherwise. In Gray and Regan's study, the oval object rotated only 90 deg so that, for a given trial, its projected shape changed either from circle to ellipse or from ellipse to circle depending on the initial orientation of the object. Thus, despite the fact that an infinite variety of optical patterns can be engendered by rotating non-spherical objects, only two types of deformation were depicted in Gray and Regan's study. For that reason, additional studies are clearly warranted.

Here we report the results of two experiments directed at estimating TTC of rotating non-spherical objects. In the first experiment, textureless, non-spherical objects rotated either about one or two axes. In the former, the distance between the two end points along the axis of rotation could be used to define local tau2; in the latter, no such optical pattern was available, compromising local tau2. In the second experiment, the density of object's surface texture varied, compromising local tau1.

## Experiment 1: Local Tau2

### Method

Fourteen experimentally naïve participants, all graduates (4 males and 10 females) from Keimyung University, volunteered for the experiment.

Displays were presented on a 106.7 cm (42 in.) LCD monitor subtending a field of view of 63.7° H × 38.9° V when viewed at a distance of 75 cm. Displays simulated a projectile approaching the observer along the sagittal plane parallel to the ground plane. The object was an ellipsoid (either a disk-shaped object or a rugby ball-shaped object) with its three semi-axes of different lengths.

Five variables were controlled. The values of TTC varied among 1.8, 3.0, 4.2, and 5.4 s and were further jittered within ± 0.2 s to minimize response bias. The four TTC values were combined with two approach velocities of 6.0 and 9.0 m/s to determine the starting location of each object. The duration of the approach also varied within a range of 2.5 ± 0.25 s. The object rotated about one axis (either the vertical or horizontal axis) or about two axes, and completed a quarter turn (90 deg), a half turn (180 deg), or a full turn (360 deg), during its approach.

The combined effects of rotation (i.e., axis and amount of rotation) were various patterns of deformation on the non-spherical objects but negligible deformation on the spherical (control) objects, which were included because they can engender reliable local tau2. The spherical objects, therefore, were controlled by TTC and velocity only, with each combination repeating three times for a total of 24 trials. These manipulations yielded a 2 (Velocity: 6 or 9 m/s) × 4 (TTC: 1.8, 3.0, 4.2, or 5.4 s) × 2 (Object Type: Disk or Rugby ball) × 3 (Amount of Rotation: quarter, half, or full turn) × 3 (Axis of Rotation: Vertical, Horizontal, or Vertical + Horizontal) design with a total of 144 trials with non-spherical objects plus 24 trials with spherical objects. All variables were controlled within-subjects.

Trials were initiated when the participant pressed the space bar to trigger the display. On termination of the display, participants were asked to predict when the object would reach them had it kept coming at the same speed and to press a key on the keyboard at the moment that coincided with their predicted time of the object's arrival. Feedback was provided throughout the experiment.

## Results and Discussion

Best fit lines were computed by regressing perceived against actual TTC for each object type. The analyses yielded regression equations: $y = 0.52 x + 1.27$ for disk, $y = 0.59 x + 1.39$ for rugby ball, and $y = 0.65 x + 0.85$ for sphere. Slopes of 0.52 and 0.59 in the non-spherical object conditions were comparable to those reported in similar TTC studies (e.g., 0.57 for inexperienced drivers reported by Cavallo & Laurent, 1988; 0.61 by Schiff & Detwiler, 1979).

Correlations were obtained between actual TTC and perceived TTC in each condition of rotation axis for each participant. The results were entered into an analysis of variance (ANOVA). The group effect was not significant, $F(2, 26) <$ 1.

These results demonstrated that human observers can perceive the TTC of rotating non-spherical objects, although less reliably, than that of spherical objects. Feedback may have facilitated participants' TTC judgments. Nevertheless, the results are remarkable considering the fact that local tau2, a possible source of TTC information in this experiment, was severely compromised with non-systematically deforming contours.

## Experiment 2: Local Tau1

### Method

Fourteen undergraduates and graduates (5 males and 9 females) from Keimyung University participated in the experiment for a nominal fee.

The same apparatus, viewing geometry, and procedure used in Experiment 1 were used. Objects were depicted with random dots whose density varied among 4, 16, 64, and 256. Because these objects were volumetric, roughly half of the surface dots were projected to the observation point.

Five variables were controlled. The values of TTC varied among 1.8, 3.6, and 5.4 s and were further jittered within ± 0.2 s. Approach velocity varied within a range of 7.5 ± 1.0 m/s; the duration of the approach varied within a range of 2.5 ± 0.25 s. As in Experiment 1, objects rotated in three different ways, that is, about one axis (either the vertical or horizontal axis) or about two axes, and underwent either a half turn (180 deg) or a full turn (360 deg). These manipulations yielded a 4 (Dot Density) × 3 (TTC) × 3 (Object) × 2 (Amount of Rotation) × 3 (Axis of Rotation) design for a total of 216 completely randomized trials. All variables were controlled within-subjects.

### Results and Discussion

Performance in each condition of dot density can be described by regression equations: $y = 0.72 x + 0.71$ for the 256 dot condition, $y = 0.65 x + 0.93$ for the 64 dot condition, $y = 0.58 x + 1.38$ for the 16 dot condition, and $y = 0.44 x + 2.50$ for the 4 dot condition, respectively. The slope for the 4 dot condition was substantially lower than those of the other three higher density conditions.

For further analysis, correlations were obtained between actual TTC and perceived TTC in each condition of dot density for each participant. The results were entered into an ANOVA. The effect of dot density was significant, $F(3, 39)$ = 24.44, $p < .0001$. The mean correlation for the 4 dot condition ($M = .49$) differed from the means of the three higher density conditions ($M = .77$ for 256 dots, $M = .71$ for 64 dots, and $M = .66$ for 16 dots). Despite the degraded performance in the 4 dot condition, the correlation coefficients of the 14 participants all reached significance. These results indicate that participants were still capable of estimating TTC, albeit to a limited degree. Note that in the 4 dot condition, only about 2 dots were projected to the observation point and these were displaced or even disappeared and were replaced by dots hidden behind due to rotation. It appears, therefore, that the visual system responds to even the slightest indication of optical expansion to extract requisite information, such as local tau1.

## General Discussion

Two experiments were directed at the perceptual capacity to estimate TTC of an approaching object even under severely perturbed or impoverished optic flow, condition intended to compromise sources of TTC information, in particular, local tau1 and local tau2. The results demonstrated that human observers are capable of estimating TTC even under severely compromised conditions, responding to even the slightest indication of optical expansion to estimate TTC of approaching objects.

## References

Cavallo, V., & Laurent, M. (1988). Visual information and skill level in time-to-collision estimation. *Perception, 17*, 623-632.

Gray, R., & Regan, D. (2000). Estimating time to collision with a rotating non-spherical object. *Vision Research, 40*, 49-63.

Schiff, W., & Detwiler, M. L. (1979). Information used in judging impending collision. *Perception, 8*, 647-58.

Tresilian, J. R. (1991). Empirical and theoretical issues in the perception of time to contact. *Journal of Experimental Psychology: Human Perception and Performance, 17*, 865-876.

*Acknowledgements.* This research is supported by a Korea Research Foundation grant (KRF-2008-327-H00020) awarded to Nam-Gyoon Kim.

*Studies in Perception & Action X*
J. B. Wagman & C. C. Pagano (Eds.)
© 2009 Taylor & Francis Group, LLC

# Analyses of User's Action for Perceiving Shapes Using an Active Perception Device

Ryo Mizuno[1], Kiyohide Ito[2], & Makoto Okamoto[2]

[1] Graduate school of System Information Science, Future University-Hakodate, JAPAN
[2] School of System Information Science, Future University-Hakodate, JAPAN

In recent years, there has been great progress in the development of sensor technology for assisting persons in the perception of their environment. Such devices obtain data and transmit it to user, and this data must be provided as meaningful information to the user. Therefore, such sensing device should be designed with human perceptual capability in mind. Humans pick up information from their environment by employing perceptual systems (Reed & Jones, 1982). Therefore, if a sensing device is to aid the perception of the user, should also be able to move in a way that mimics perceptual systems. Mizuno, Ito, Akita, Ono, Komatsu & Okamoto (2008) called such moveable sensing devices "Active Perception Devices".

Palmsonar is one such active perception device. It is used specifically to aid perception of environmental properties in the visually impaired. Palmsonar measures the distance between the user and an object by an ultrasonic sensor and transmits this information through vibrations applied to the user's palm. Palmsonar not only measures and transmits the distance between a user and an object, but also aids in perception of the shapes of the objects without vision.

We conducted two experiments that compared how expert and novice users use the Palmsonar in a shape perception task.

## Experiment 1

Experiment 1 investigated the ability of novice participants to use the Palmsonar to perceive shape.

### Method

Participants were nine university students. They had never used Palmsonar prior to the experiment. They were blindfolded. Participants used the Palmsonar to explore four shapes—"sphere", "cube", "rectangular solid", and "cylinder" while maintaining a 1.5 m radius from each shape. Objects surfaces were constructed from paper. The volume of each object was 47,713 cm$^3$.

The task of the participant was to report the perceived shape of each object. Objects were presented randomly. There were 32 trials consisting of eight trials for each of the four objects. Before the experimental trials, there were training trials. In training trials, there were two shapes: "cone" and "triangle pole". Trials lasted 2 minutes.

### Results and Discussion

The mean percentage of correct identification for the sphere, cube, rectangular solid, and cylinder were 27.78, 51.94, 30.56, 26.39, respectively. A percentage response matrix for this experiment can be seen in Table 1. T-tests compared the mean percentage of correct identification for each shape relative to the chance level. Results of the T-test shows that performance with cube was better than chance, $t(16) = 2.80$, $p < .05$ level. By contrast, performance with sphere, rectangular solid and cylinder was not significantly better than chance level. These results indicate that shape identification is quite difficult for novice perceivers, and shapes with sharp edges are more easily identified than shapes with smooth edges.

Table 1. Mean percentage of responses for each shape

|             | SPHERE | CUBE  | RECTANGULAR | CYLINDER |
|-------------|--------|-------|-------------|----------|
| SPHERE      | 27.78  | 31.54 | 22.22       | 44.44    |
| CUBE        | 11.11  | 51.94 | 37.50       | 19.44    |
| RECTANGULAR | 11.11  | 12.50 | 30.56       | 9.72     |
| CYLINDER    | 50.00  | 4.17  | 9.72        | 26.39    |

### Experiment 2

The purpose of this experiment is to investigate difference in the movements used by experts and novices in perceiving shape using Palmsonar.

### Method

The participants were an expert and a novice at shape identification using Palmsonar. The expert had trained shape identification for 3 days (2 hours/day). In training trials, there were two shapes: "cone" and "triangle pole". The novice participant had never used Palmsonar prior to this experiment. The expert and the novice were university students. Materials and procedure were the same as experiment 1. In this experiment, the user's movements were captured by two video cameras and motion capture system (PV Studio 3D). The 16 trials consisted of four trials for each of the four objects.

**Results and Discussion**

The percentage of correct identification by expert and novice were 87.5 and 31.3 respectively. Analysis of movement data focused on a) The regularity of sensor's motion at vertical direction, b) changes in amplitude in time series, c) differences in amplitude among each body part. Figure 1 shows wave patterns of expert and novice at horizontal direction.

First, the auto correlation coefficient was calculated in order to verify the regularity of sensor's motion at vertical direction. Figure 2 presents the auto correlation function of series of sensor's position at vertical direction. The mean of square values of auto correlation efficient ($r^2$) were compared in a T-test. The auto correlation efficient at highest point of expert's motion is higher than novice's motion significantly, $t(15) = 4.54$, $p < .01$. This suggests that regularity of motion at vertical direction is effective for shape identification.

Next, in order to verify changes of amplitude in time series, time series were divided three phases, and standard deviation (SD) of sensor position at horizontal direction were calculated in each phase (see Figure 2). In the case of novice, SD increased over time (1.29, 1.28, 1.57). To the contrary, in the case of expert, SD decreased over time (1.39, 0.92, 0.79). T-tests compared the mean standard deviation for each phase of expert with novice's. In the first phase, there was no difference between them. At middle phase and final phase, the SD of the expert's was smaller than that of the novice (Middle phase: $t(26) = -2.35$, $p < .02$, Final phase: $t(26) = -3.96$, p < .001). This result indicates that experts move the sensor slowly decrease the variability with which they move the sensor over time. In other words, effective search of information for shape perception using an active sensing device is to change moving sensor from rough search to detail search.

Finally, the mean SD of each position of body parts and sensor at horizontal direction were calculated. In the case of expert, SD of the sensor, wrist, elbow, and shoulder were 1.63, 1.64, 1.71, and 1.83 respectively. In the case of novice, SD of the sensor, wrist, elbow, and shoulder were 2.06, 1.9, 1.57, and 1.49 respectively (see Figure 3). In general, the movements of the novice had greater variability than those of the expert.

*Mizuno, Ito, & Okamoto*

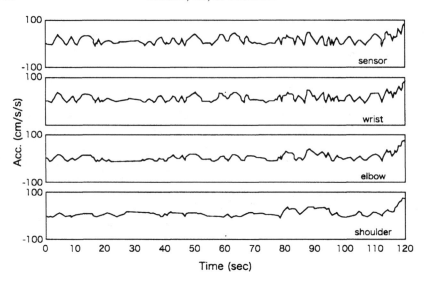

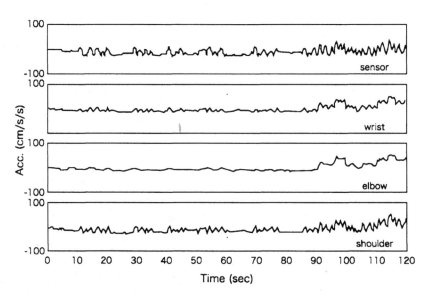

*Figure 1.* User's motion for expert (top) and novice (bottom)

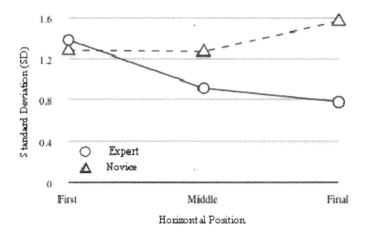

*Figure 2.* SD in horizontal direction

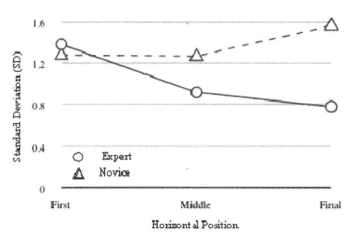

*Figure 3.* SD of each body part and sensor

## References

Mizuno, R., Ito, K., Akita, J., Ono, T., Komatsu, T., & Okamoto, M. (2008). Shape Perception using CyARM - Active Sensing Device. *International Conference of Cognitive Science 2008*, 182-185.

Reed, E., & Jones, R. (1982). *Reasons for Realism*. Lawrence Erlbaum Associates.

*Studies in Perception & Action X*
J. B. Wagman & C. C. Pagano (Eds.)
© 2009 Taylor & Francis Group, LLC

# Improvements in Perceptual Accuracy Scale to Frequency of Feedback about Task Performance

Jeffrey B. Wagman & Dawn M. McBride

Department of Psychology, Illinois State University

Perceptual learning is the improvement of perceptual skill with practice (E. Gibson, 1969). In general, perceptual consistency improves with repeated perceptual experience regardless of whether that experience includes any information about task performance (Wagman et al., 2001). However, perceptual accuracy improves only when such experience includes information about how perceived values compare to actual values (Withagen & Michaels, 2005).

A recent study by Wagman et al. (2008) compared post-test improvements in perceptual accuracy when perceivers were provided with feedback about task performance (knowledge of results, or KR) on different proportions of trials during a practice session. In this study, participants reported the perceived length of wielded occluded T-shaped objects in a pre-test, practice session, and post-test. This study resulted in three important findings. First, consistent with previous research, there were post-test improvements in perceptual accuracy (defined in terms of changes in slope and intercept of the regression lines relating perceived length to actual length) only when KR was provided during practice trials. Second, such improvements occurred even when KR was only provided on a portion of practice trials. In particular, post-test perceptual accuracy improved when KR was presented on 100% of practice trials and when KR was provided on 50% of practice trials but not when KR was presented on 25% or 12.5% of practice trials. Third, there was no difference in post-test improvements when KR was presented on 100% of practice trials and when KR was provided on 50% of practice trials.

In short, the results suggest that in this task, (a) providing KR on 50% of practice trials was as effective in bringing about improvements in perceptual accuracy as providing KR on 100% of practice trials and (b) providing KR on 25% of practice trials was as ineffective in bringing about such improvements as providing KR on 0% of practice trials. In other words, the results seem to establish endpoints at which the embedding of KR during practice is effective at improving post-test perceptual accuracy (and at which the embedding of KR is ineffective at doing so). The current experiment is an attempt to further these findings by investigating such improvements (or the lack thereof) when the embedding of KR in a practice session falls between these endpoints.

**Method**

One hundred four (104) students from Illinois State University participated in this experiment. They were randomly assigned to one of seven KR conditions (.50, .46, .42, .38, .33, .29, and .25KR). The number preceding the KR refers to the proportion of KR trials provided in the practice session. The experiment consisted of a pre-test, practice session, and post-test.

In the pre-test, participants wielded occluded T-shaped objects and reported the perceived length of each object by means of magnitude production (i.e., by adjusting a moveable flag to correspond to the perceived length of the object). Six objects were wielded four times each, and the order of presentation of objects was randomized. In the practice session, participants performed the same task using a different set of six T- shaped objects. The practice session consisted of two different types of trials—KR and No-KR. No-KR trials proceeded as in the pre-test. KR-trials proceeded in the same way except that after a participant provided their perceptual report, the experimenter readjusted the distance of the flag to correspond to the actual length of the object. The number of KR-trials in the practice session depended on the experimental condition. There were twelve KR-trials in the 0.50KR condition, eleven in the 0.46KR condition, ten in the 0.42KR condition, nine in the 0.38KR condition, eight in the .33KR condition, seven in the .29KR condition, and six in the .25KR condition. KR-trials were distributed as evenly as possible across the practice session. The post-test proceeded exactly as the pre-test.

**Results and Discussion**

For each participant, we computed regression lines with perceived length as the dependent variable and actual length as the independent variable in both the pre-test and post-test. We then calculated difference scores for the slope and intercept of the regression lines for each participant. Given that we expected slopes to *increase* from pre-test to post-test (slopes in the pre-test tended to be less than 1.0), difference scores for slope were calculated by subtracting pre-test values from post-test values. Given that we expected intercept to *decrease* from pre-test to post-test (intercepts in the pre-test tended to be greater than 0.0), differences scores for intercept were calculated by subtracting post-test values from pre-test values.

A one-sample t-test found that difference scores for slope ($M$ = .24) were greater than 0 [$t(103)$ = 11.37, $p < .001$] (i.e., slopes tended to increase from pre-test to post-test). However, a one-way ANOVA found no differences among difference scores for slope across the seven KR conditions [$F(6,97)$ = 1.60, $p$ = .16]. Similarly, a one-sample t-test found that difference scores for intercept ($M$ = 8.1) were also greater than 0 [$t(103)$ = 9.43, $p < .001$] (i.e. intercepts tended to decrease from pre-test to post-test). However, a one-way ANOVA found no differences among difference scores for intercept across the seven KR conditions [$F < 1$]. In summary, the results suggest that perceptual accuracy improved from pre-test to post-test and that the degree of improvement did not differ across KR conditions.

The findings that (a) the degree of improvement in perceptual accuracy did not vary across KR conditions and (b) post-test perceptual accuracy improved when KR was provided on 25% of practice trials are somewhat contrary to those of Wagman et al. (2008). As a result, we made an attempt to explicitly compare the results of the two studies. We calculated difference scores for the slopes and intercepts reported by Wagman et al. (in the same manner as in the current experiment) and created learning curves (for slope and intercept, respectively) using the difference scores from both experiments (see Figures 1 and 2).

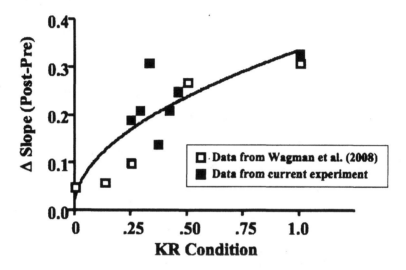

*Figure 1.* A power law function accounted for 69% of the variance in slope difference scores when the data from the current experiment were combined with the data from Wagman et al. (2008).

In each case, a power law function provided a better fit of the resultant learning curve than an exponential function. The power law function accounted for 69% of the variance in slope difference scores and 63% of the variance in intercept difference scores (see Figure 1 and Figure 2). Such findings suggest that across experiments, perceptual accuracy improves at a rate that is mathematically scaled to the frequency with which the perceiver is provided with information about task performance and suggests that like many other cognitive, motor, and perceptual skills, perceptual learning exhibits power law structure (see J. Anderson, 2000, for a review).

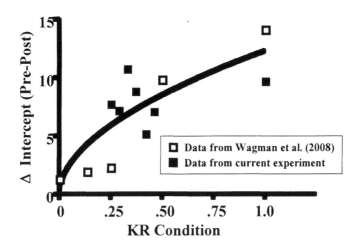

*Figure 2.* A power law function accounted for 63% of the variance in intercept difference scores when the data from the current experiment were combined with the data from Wagman et al. (2008).

## References

Anderson, J. R. (2000). *Learning and memory*. New York: Wiley.

Gibson, E. J. (1969). *Principles of perceptual learning and development*. New York: Appleton.

Wagman, J. B., Shockley, K., Riley, M. A., & Turvey, M. T. (2001) Attunement, calibration, and exploration in fast haptic perceptual learning. *Journal of Motor Behavior, 33*(4) 323-327.

Wagman, J. B., McBride, D. M., & Trefzger, A. J. (2008). Perceptual experience and post-test improvements in perceptual accuracy. *Perception & Psychophysics, 70*, 1060-1067.

Withagen, R. & Michaels, C. F. (2005). The role of feedback information for calibration and attunement in perceiving length by dynamic touch. *Journal of Experimental Psychology: Human Perception & Performance, 31*, 1379-1390.

*Acknowledgements.* We thank Jeremy Orr and Alex Gomory for help with data collection

*Studies in Perception & Action X*
J. B. Wagman & C. C. Pagano (Eds.)
© 2009 Taylor & Francis Group, LLC

# The Influence of Eyeheight and Optic flow on Egocentric Distance Perception

Jonathan Shook, Eliah White, & Kevin Shockley

University of Cincinnati, Cincinnati, OH USA

Perception of extent in the environment has been shown to be a function of the effective eyeheight of an observer—the height from the line of sight to the ground. Ooi and He (2007) proposed that distances may be coded in terms of the angle subtended between the extent on the ground scaled to one's eyeheight. (cf. Mark, 1987; Warren & Whang, 1987; Wraga & Proffitt, 2000, for similar scaling of environmental layout in other spatial dimensions). In other words, if one is given a target distance (i.e., extent) to be reported, one will report in terms of the angle subtended which corresponds to different extents as eyeheight changes.

Perception of distance, however, has also been shown to be a function of optic flow. Changes in optic flow velocity (i.e. the rate of flow of texture elements in one's field of view) while walking on a treadmill have been shown to affect egocentric distance estimations (i.e., perceived self-motion) (e.g., Proffitt 2003). This general phenomenon has been attributed to calibration between visual and kinesthetic information about forward motion (e.g., Rieser, Pick, Ashmead, & Garing, 1995). At issue is the visual information about forward motion that is scaled to kinesthetic information about forward motion. One possibility is optic flow velocity (a global measure of the rate of optic flow in one's field of view). However, all of the texture elements in an observer's field of view do not transform in a uniform fashion. Elements which are closer to the observer flow by the observer at a faster rate than elements farther away. Imagine an observer walking down a hallway. Texture elements on the ground will flow by faster for a short observer than for a tall observer, while elements on the walls will flow by at the same rate for short and tall observers (i.e., the wall is the same distance from short and tall observers while the floor is a different distance from short and tall observers' eyes). Thus, rather than coding distance in terms of the angle subtended by an extent in the environment, distances may be coded in terms of the number of texture elements (i.e., the number of texture elements that flow by for a given number steps for a treadmill virtual reality environment).

In canonical flow fields, these two factors—angle subtended by an extent on the ground and the magnitude of optic flow on the ground plane—co-vary as a function of eyeheight. In order to disambiguate these two potential visual influences. We manipulated both the effective eyeheight of a perceiver with no change in (global) optic flow velocity in the display and the optic flow velocity in the display to produce an equivalent magnitude of optic magnitude on the ground plane for a fixed eyeheight.

## Method

Participants walked on a treadmill while wearing a virtual reality head mounted display (HMD), which depicted the observer traveling through a tunnel. The task was to walk a target distance that would be indicated by a pair of "starting position" cones and a pair of "ending position" cones (12 meters apart) depicted in the graphical display, and then reproduce that distance (i.e., magnitude production) on the next trial.

Magnitude of optic flow on the ground plan for a given optic flow velocity and eyeheight was determined according to the following equation (Warren, 1990):

$$\dot{\beta} = \frac{v}{h} \cos \alpha \sin^2 \beta$$

where $v$ is speed, $h$ is eyeheight, $\alpha$ specifies the meridian, and $\beta$ specifies the eccentricity of the line of sight (both = 90° for looking straight down at the ground), and $\beta$ (dot) is the flow magnitude expressed as a rate of change of angular position. Magnitude of optic flow on the ground plane was manipulated by pairing five levels of eyeheight (1.20, 1.10, 1.0, .90, and .80 × actual height depicted at 1.8 m) with an optic flow velocity of 1.12 m/s (2.5 mph) yielding five values of optic flow magnitude defined with respect to the ground and the observer's point of observation (0.51, 0.56, 0.61, 0.68, and 0.76 deg/s, respectively). Optic flow velocity was manipulated accordingly (1.42, 1.25, 1.12, 1.01, 0.93 m/s, respectively) with no corresponding change in eyeheight to achieve the same values of optic flow magnitude on the ground plane as in the eyeheight manipulation conditions. A constant treadmill (i.e., actual) walking speed of 1.12 m/s (2.5 mph) was used in all conditions, yielding 9 experimental conditions.

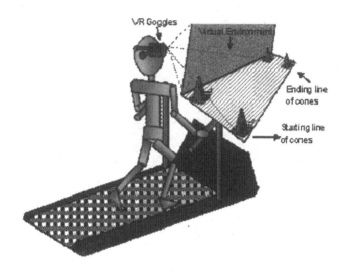

Standard Distance

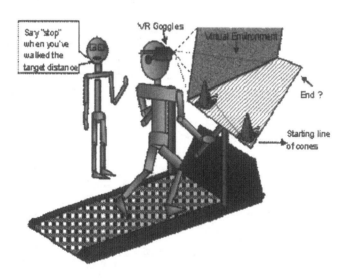

Reporting Distance

*Figure 1.* Method of presenting standard distance and reporting distance via magnitude production.

## Results and Discussion

Distance reports were submitted to a 5 (Magnitude of optic flow) × 2 (Mode of manipulation) repeated-measures analysis of variance. There was no main effect for magnitude of optic flow and no main effect of mode of manipulation, $Fs < 1$. There was, however a significant interaction between the two factors, $F(4,44) = 2.63$, $p < .05$. Post-hoc comparison showed that mode of manipulation influenced perceived distance at the optic flow magnitude of 1.1, units, $t(11) = 2.67$, $p < .05$, with the optic flow velocity manipulation showing a greater perceived distance than the eyeheight manipulation.

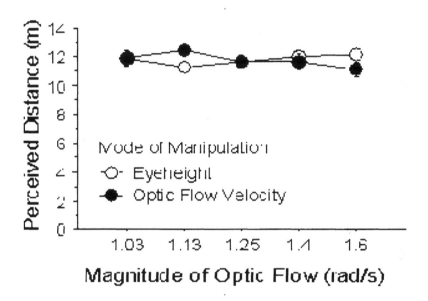

*Figure 2.* Distance perception as a function of magnitude of optic flow on the ground plane with optic flow velocity and eyeheight as modes of manipulation.

Neither manipulation of optic flow magnitude showed a systematic influence on distance perception. However, a decrease in optic flow velocity did show a significant increase in distance perception relative to the eyeheight manipulation for one magnitude of optic flow, which is consistent with previous studies showing that perceived distance increases with decreasing optic flow velocity (e.g., Proffitt et al., 2003; Mohler et al., 2004; White, 2008). The lack of a systematic influence of optic flow velocity may reflect the fact that the present study used a narrower range of optic flow velocities that other studies showing an influence of that variable. The present study showed no evidence that eyeheight influences egocentric distance reports in contrast to the results of Ooi and He (2007).

**References**

Mark, L. S. (1987). Eyeheight-scaled information about affordances: A study of sitting and stair climbing. *Journal of Experimental Psychology, 13*, 367-370.

Mohler, B. J., & Thompson, W. B. (2007). Calibration of locomotion resulting from visual motion in a treadmill-based virtual environment. *ACM Transaction on Applied Perception, 4*, 1-15.

Ooi, T. L. & He, Z. J. (2007) A distance judgment function based on space perception mechanisms – revisiting Gilinsky's (1951) equation. *Psychological Review, 114(2)*, 441-454.

Proffitt, D. R., Stefanucci, J., Banton, T., & Epstein, W. (2003). The role of effort in perceiving distance. *Psychological Science, 2*, 106-112.

Rieser, J. J., Pick, H. L., Ashmead, D. H., & Garing A. E. (1995). Calibration of human locomotion and models of perceptual-motor organization. *Journal of Experimental Psychology: Human Perception and Performance, 3*, 480-497.

Warren, W. H., Jr., & Whang, S. (1987). Visual guidance of walking through apertures: Body-scaled information for affordances. *Journal of Experimental Psychology: Human Perception and Performance, 13*, 371-383.

White, E.(2008,) *The influence of multimodally specified effort on distance perception.* Unpublished master's thesis, University of Cincinnati, Cincinnati, Ohio, USA.

Wraga, M., & Proffitt, D. R. (2000). Mapping the zone of eye height utility for seated and standing observers. *Perception, 29*, 1361-1383.

*Acknowledgements.* This research was supported by NSF grant #0716319.

*Studies in Perception & Action X*
J. B. Wagman & C. C. Pagano (Eds.)
© 2009 Taylor & Francis Group, LLC

# Chapter 4:

# Perception of Affordances

Studies in Perception & Action X
J. B. Wagman & C. C. Pagano (Eds.)
© 2009 Taylor & Francis Group, LLC

# Sensitivity to Changes in Action Capabilities

Dilip N. Athreya[1], Michael A. Riley[1], Tehran J. Davis[1],
& Veronica C. Ramenzoni[2]

[1]Department of Psychology, University of Cincinnati
[2]Department of Psychology, University of Virginia

Perception of what the environment affords is fundamental to the capacity to successfully act (Gibson, 1979; Profitt, 2006). For instance, hiking across rugged terrain or crossing a busy street requires that a person can determine a safe, traversable route and then tailor muscular forces so as to get from the start to the goal point. Many studies have documented the ability to successfully perceive affordances (for a review, see Fajen, Riley, & Tuvey, 2009).

How does this ability change as one's action capabilities change? Previously, Mark (1987) found that perceivers can retune perceived maximum sitting height after their actual maximum sitting height was modified by attaching blocks to the feet. After about eight trials, participants who wore the blocks approached perfect accuracy at perceiving maximum sitting height. Participants in a control group, who did not wear the blocks, exhibited high accuracy from the outset, and no change over trials. In a later study, Ramenzoni, Riley, Shockley, and Davis (2008) investigated perception of the maximum height to which one could jump to reach an object. Participants' initial estimates of this affordance boundary were considerably less accurate than in Mark's study—on average, participants underestimated the boundary by 14.4 cm. Ramenzoni et al. manipulated participants' jumping height by attaching weights (~5% of each participant's body mass) to the ankles, reducing jumping height by 5.71 cm, on average. When participants provided another set of estimates of the affordance boundary after walking while wearing the ankle weights, they reported a lower maximum jumping-reach height than was reported by control-group participants who were not encumbered by weights. Participants who wore the weights appeared immediately sensitive to the change in their action capabilities—initial afffordance boundary estimates were reduced by 6.53 cm, on average, a value close to the actual change in their action capabilities. However, despite the sensitivity to the amount of change in their action capabilities, participants still underestimated their maximum jumping-reach height by, on average, 16.2 cm. Participants were not given the opportunity to recalibrate their estimates.

Davis, Ramenzoni, Shockley, and Riley (2008) found that with repeated opportunities to provide perceptual reports participants' initial underestimations of maximum jumping-reach height became more accurate, even without feedback about accuracy. Davis et al. did not investigate the consequences of modifying the perceiver's action capabilities, however. The goal of this study was to determine whether perceivers would come to exhibit improved accuracy in reports of maximum jumping-reach height after modification of their action capabilities.

## Method

### Participants

40 University of Cincinnati undergraduates participated in exchange for course credit. Participants were randomly assigned to either the control (no weights) or experimental (weights attached) group. All participants had normal or corrected-to-normal vision.

### Apparatus

Participants estimated the ability to jump and reach to grasp a small, plastic cylinder (5 cm diameter × 4 cm) suspended from the ceiling via a pulley by a nylon rope 22 cm in front of a perpendicular background surface covered in black felt (250 cm tall × 96 cm wide). One Reebok exercise weight was attached to the ankle of each of the experimental group participants' legs. Each weight was adjusted between 2.67 kg and 4.54 kg in 0.23 kg increments by adding or removing masses from pockets so that the weights totaled ~5% of each participant's body mass.

### Procedure

Maximum jumping-reach height was defined as a vertical power jump, executed from a standing position with bending of the knees allowed but without an approach step, that would allow for the cylinder to be grasped at the peak of the jump with the preferred arm extended overhead. Actual maximum jumping-reach height was measured after the experiment. Participants performed three jumps without the weights and (for the experimental group) three while wearing the weights. Jump heights for the three trials were respectively averaged to obtain actual maximum jumping-reach height without and with the weights.

Participants in the experimental and control groups were asked to estimate their maximum jumping-reach height. Estimates were obtained before and after walking with weights (24 laps around a table in the laboratory, maintaining a constant pace), with blocks of four trials conducted before and then again after the walking period. For experimental group participants, the before-walking estimates were obtained before they wore the ankle weights, which were attached prior to the walking period. After walking the specified amount, participants returned to the previous position and made the after-walking estimates (for which experimental group participants wore the weights).

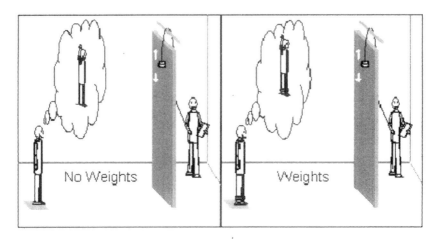

*Figure 1.* Illustration of experimental set-up and procedure.

Estimates of maximum jumping-reach height were obtained using the method of adjustments. Participants verbally instructed an experimenter (who stood out of sight behind the apparatus) to raise or lower the object (randomized for each trial; a trial consisted of a pair of up-down presentations that was averaged to obtain a single perceptual report) by means of the rope and pulley until the object was just at the perceived maximum jumping-reach height. Between trials, participants closed their eyes while the experimenter reset the apparatus. Participants were not allowed to jump or stand and reach in front of the apparatus until data collection was completed.

**Results and Discussion**

A 2 (experimental/control group) × 2 (before/after walking) × 4 (trials) analysis of variance (ANOVA) showed significant differences for raw perceptual estimates before and after walking, $F(1, 38) = 5.54$, $p < .05$. However, this effect disappeared when the ratio of perceived to actual maximum jumping-reach height was analyzed, with the experimental group's after-walking estimates scaled by their jumping height with weights ($F < 1$). This indicates that participants were equally accurate at perceiving the affordance boundary before and after their action capabilities were altered. Analysis of the raw perceptual reports also indicated a marginally significant interaction group × walking interaction, $F(1, 38) - 3.78$, $p - .059$ (see Figure 2).

Our results are similar to the Ramenzoni et al. results. Participants did not exhibit improved accuracy in their reports of maximum jumping-reach height after modification of their action capabilities. In contrast to Mark's (1987) results, our results show an immediate calibration in perceptual judgments based on new bodily capabilities, though participants consistently underestimated.

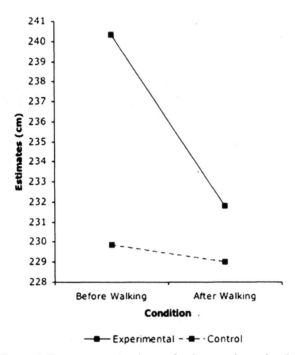

*Figure 2.* Raw perceptual estimates for the experimental and control groups before and after walking. For the experimental group, the after-walking estimates were made while the wearing ankle weights.

## References

Davis, T. J., Ramenzoni, V. C., Shockley, K., & Riley, M. A. (2008). Tuning in to another agent's action capabilities. *CogSci 2008: Proceedings of the 30ᵗʰ Annual Meeting of the Cognitive Science Society.*

Fajen, B. R., Riley, M. A., & Turvey, M. T. (2009). Information, affordances, and the control of action in sport. *International Journal of Sport Psychology, 40,* 79-107.

Gibson, J. J. (1979). *The ecological approach to visual perception.* Boston, Houghton Mifflin

Proffitt, D. R. (2006). Embodied perception and the economy of action. *Perspectives on Psychological Science, 1,* 110-122.

Ramenzoni, V. C., Riley, M. A., Shockley, K., & Davis, T. (2008). Carrying the height of the world on your ankles: Encumbered observers reduce estimates of how high an actor can jump. *Quarterly Journal of Experimental Psychology, 61,* 1487-1495.

*Studies in Perception & Action X*
J. B. Wagman & C. C. Pagano (Eds.)
© 2009 Taylor & Francis Group, LLC

# Understanding the Dynamics of Behavioral Transitions in Affordance Experiments

Stacy Lopresti-Goodman[1], T.D. Frank[1], M. J. Richardson[2], & M.T. Turvey[1]

[1]CESPA, University of Connecticut, Storrs, CT
[2]Colby College, Waterville, ME

To perceive an opportunity for action presumes that one perceives the environment relative to one's dimensions and capabilities (Gibson, 1979/1986). For example, an object that affords grasping with one hand by an adult, affords grasping with two hands by a small child. Despite different action capabilities of differently sized individuals, an invariant object-size/hand-size ratio (a $\pi$ - number) seems to specify the boundary between one- to two-hand grasping. It is the case, however, that the boundary differs experimentally for systematically increasing and systematically decreasing object/hand ratios. There is hysteresis (Lopresti-Goodman, Richardson, et al., 2009). Here we derive parameter estimations for a dynamical model (Frank, Richardson et al., in press) of this hysteresis effect which is based on a model first introduced by Haken (1991).

Let the order parameters $\xi_1$ and $\xi_2$ represent the generalized amplitudes of the one- and two-hand grasping modes, respectively. $\xi_1 > 0$, $\xi_2 = 0$ defines the one-hand mode, $\xi_2 > 0$, $\xi_1 = 0$ defines the two-hand mode. Then, the grasping behavior is determined by the time evolution of $\xi_1$ and $\xi_2$:

$$\dot{\xi}_1(t) = \lambda_1\xi_1 - B\xi_2^2\xi_1 - C(\xi_1^2 + \xi_2^2)\xi_1 \tag{1}$$
$$\dot{\xi}_2(t) = \lambda_2\xi_2 - B\xi_1^2\xi_2 - C(\xi_1^2 + \xi_2^2)\xi_2 \tag{2}$$

In (1) and (2), $\lambda_1$ and $\lambda_2$ are the one- and two-hand (so-called attention) parameters, respectively, corresponding to $\xi_1$ and $\xi_2$. By Eq. 12 in Frank et al., $\lambda_1$ and $\lambda_2$ relate linearly to the object/hand ratio ($\alpha$) which acts as the control parameter (van der Kamp, Savelsbergh, & Davis, 1998).

$$\lambda_1 = \beta(L_{1,0} - \alpha) \tag{3}$$
$$\lambda_2 = \beta(L_{2,0} + \alpha) \tag{4}$$

where $\beta$ determines the overall size of $\lambda$. From Eq. 9 in Frank et al. we see that

$$B = C(g-1) \tag{5}$$

With some simple substitutions, Eqs. 1 and 2 become

$$\dot{\xi}_1(t) = \lambda_1 \xi_1 - Cg\xi_2^2 \xi_1 - C\xi_1^3 \tag{6}$$
$$\dot{\xi}_2(t) = \lambda_2 \xi_2 - Cg\xi_1^2 \xi_2 - C\xi_2^3 \tag{7}$$

with $g$ representing the strength of the interaction between the two grasping modes and the stability of their attractors.

Estimates of $L_{1,0}$, $L_{2,0}$, and $g$ can be derived from Lopresti-Goodman et al., (2009). They investigated the task of grasping and moving light wooden planks of different sizes using either one or two hands. In their Experiment 2, they found that speed of object presentation (Slow: 10 s/plank and Fast: 3 s/plank), and cognitive load (Load: counting backwards aloud by 7, or No Load: Not counting) affected the degree of hysteresis.

Given the physical constraint at $\alpha = 1$ in the ascending sequence, forcing a switch from one- to two-hands, we will set $L_{1,0} = 1$. Parameter values for $L_{2,0}$ and $g$ can then be derived from Lopresti-Goodman et al.'s experimental observations of the transition points for the ascending ($\alpha_{c,2}$) and descending ($\alpha_{c,1}$) sequences. Eq. 13 of Frank et al. yields

$$g = (1 - \alpha_{c,1})/(1 - \alpha_{c,2}) \tag{8}$$

Furthermore, a detailed analysis shows (see Eq. 10 below) that $g$ increases when the difference between the $\alpha_c$ values ($\Delta\alpha_c = \alpha_{c,2} - \alpha_{c,1}$) increases, provided that $L_{2,0}$ is constant. That is, $g$ is related to degree of hysteresis.

A qualitative analysis of the Lopresti-Goodman et al. data revealed that hysteresis is exaggerated with increased constraints on the system. Accordingly, we expect $g$ to be influenced by the level of task-difficulty, and should be larger for those conditions in which participants experienced a fast presentation speed or a cognitive load. A 2 (Speed: slow or fast) × 2(Cognitive Load: no load or load) Univariate ANOVA revealed a significant effect of Speed, $F(1, 44) = 6.28$, $p < 0.05$, indicating that $g$ for the fast-paced condition ($M = 1.91 \pm 0.85$) was significantly larger than $g$ for the slow-paced condition ($M = 1.37 \pm 0.60$). There was no significant differences for the different Cognitive Load conditions ($M_{Load} = 1.79 \pm 0.69$ and $M_{No\ Load} = 1.49 \pm 0.84$), nor was there a significant Speed × Cognitive Load interaction, $F < 1.0$. Since $g$ determines the strength of the interaction between the two grasping modes, as well as the strength of the two modes' attractors, we may infer that increasing the speed of object presentation increases the interaction between the two grasping modes.

With regard to the $L_{2,0}$ parameter, an analysis of Eq. 13 of the Frank et al. paper yields

$$L_{2,0} = 1 - \alpha_{c,1} - \alpha_{c,2} \tag{9}$$

Since $L_{2,0}$ also depends upon the size of $\Delta\alpha_c$, we expect task-difficulty to influence its value. Specifically, when task-difficulty increases, $L_{2,0}$ may also increase indicating that the two-hand mode represents a more stable form of behavior for more difficult tasks. Therefore, increased values of $L_{2,0}$ should result in participants using the two-hand mode more often. A qualitative analysis of the Lopresti-Goodman et al. data revealed, however, that this is not the case. Instead, the significant Sequence × Speed and Sequence × Load interactions indicate that participants only used the two-hand mode more often in the descending sequences. Specifically, $\alpha_{c,1}$ decreased with increases in task-difficulty, whereas $\alpha_{c,2}$ was invariant regardless of the condition; therefore we may not expect significant differences on $L_{2,0}$ for the different levels of task-difficulty.

A Univariate ANOVA revealed that there was no effect of Speed, $F(1, 44) = 2.79, p > 0.05$, Cognitive Load, $F < 1.00$, nor an interaction between the two, $F < 1.00$. Despite the lack of significant differences, qualitatively $L_{2,0}$ was larger in the fast-paced ($M = -0.29 \pm 0.18$) and cognitive load ($M = -0.27 \pm 0.17$) conditions than in the slow-paced ($M = -0.34 \pm 0.20$) or no load ($M = -0.36 \pm 0.21$) conditions. These results suggest that $g$ and $L_{2,0}$ interact and simultaneously change with increases in task difficulty. An analysis in the $g \times L_{2,0}$ two-dimensional space may reveal differences in where these parameter values cluster. For example, low levels of task difficulty may result in $g$ and $L_{2,0}$ values clustering near the origin, while increased levels of task difficulty may result in clusters farther from this point. Since we know that hysteresis size ($\Delta\alpha_c$) is influenced by task difficulty, we will plot $g$ and $L_{2,0}$ on contour lines for which $\Delta\alpha_c$ is constant (Figure 1).

$$\Delta\alpha_c = (g - 1)(1 + L_{2,0})/(g + 1) \tag{10}$$

For each data point, we have calculated the signed minimal distance from the contour line representing $\Delta\alpha_c > 0$. A Univariate ANOVA revealed a significant effect of Speed, $F(1, 44) = 6.87, p < 0.05$, with the parameter values for the slow-paced condition clustering below this line ($M = -0.09 \pm 0.35$) and the fast-paced condition clustering above it ($M = 0.19 \pm 0.42$). There was also a significant effect of Cognitive Load, $F(1, 44) = 6.43, p < 0.05$, with parameter values for the no-load condition clustering below the contour line ($M = -0.89 \pm 0.43$) and for the load condition clustering above it ($M - 0.19 \pm 0.37$). There was no significant Speed × Cognitive Load interaction, $F < 1.00$.

In conclusion, we have demonstrated with the parameter derivations for the Frank et al. model that affordances fit within a dynamical systems framework. Additionally, we have shown that differing levels of task difficulty influence the interaction between the two possible grasping modes and the strengths of their corresponding attractors. Future empirical work will focus on testing predictions the model makes about the influence of other levels of task difficulty.

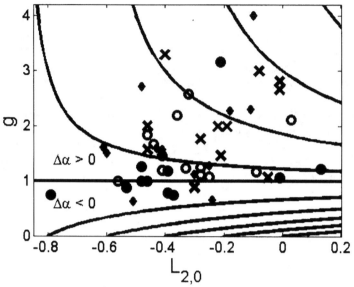

*Figure 1.* Solid black circles represent participants in the slow-speed no-load condition, solid white the slow-speed cognitive condition, black diamonds the fast-speed no-load condition and ×s represent the fast-speed cognitive condition. The first contour line, representing $\Delta\alpha_c > 0$, was used to calculate the signed minimal distances.

### References

Frank, T. D., Richardson, M. J., Lopresti-Goodman, S. M., & Turvey, M. T. (in press). Order parameter dynamics of body-scaled hysteresis and mode transitions in grasping behavior. *Journal of Biological Physics.*

Gibson, J. J. (1979). *The ecological approach to visual perception.* Boston: Houghton Mifflin.

Haken, H. (1991) *Synergetic computers and cognition*, Springer, Berlin

Lopresti-Goodman, S. M., Richardson, M. J., Baron, R. M., Carello, C., & Marsh, K. L. (2009). Task constraints and affordance boundaries. *Motor Control, 13*, 69-83.

van der Kamp, J., Savelsbergh, G. J. P., & Davis, W. E. (1998). Body-scaled ratio as a control parameter for prehension in 5- to 9-year-old children. *Developmental Psychobiology, 33*(4), 351-361.

*Studies in Perception & Action X*
J. B. Wagman & C. C. Pagano (Eds.)
© 2009 Taylor & Francis Group, LLC

# Differences between American and Chinese Students in Perceiving Multiple Affordances for Common Objects

Lin Ye, Wilson Cardwell, Stephanie Karges,
Milena Petrovic, & Leonard S. Mark

Department of Psychology, Miami University, Oxford, Ohio

Previous work has shown that perceiving one of an object's nondesigned (i.e., not the primary use for which an object was designed) uses reduces the likelihood of detecting another nondesigned use for that object (Ye, et al., 2006). Participants were shown a collection of nine objects. Some objects had only affordance 1 ($O_{AFF\ 1}$) (e.g., *pound-able-with*); other objects had only affordance 2 (e.g., *scoop-able-with*) ($O_{AFF\ 2}$); the remaining objects had both affordances 1 and 2 ($O_{AFF\ 1\&2}$). For Task 1, participants identified all of the objects with affordance 1. Immediately following the completion of the first task, participants performed Task 2, in which they identified objects with affordance 2, which included objects with both affordances as well as objects with only affordance 2. Ye et al. (2006) found that on Task 2, participants were more likely to identify objects with only affordance 2 than objects with both affordances that had previously been identified as having affordance 1 on the first task. In a follow up study with students from China who were studying in the United States, the difference between $O_{AFF\ 2}$ and $O_{AFF1\&2}$ was significantly smaller on Task 2 than for American college students. Figure 1 summarizes these initial findings. This difference was not unexpected because in the Chinese culture people typically find multiple uses for a single object, unlike in the United States, where people tend to favor special purpose tools that are optimal for performing a particular function. For example, whereas Americans have special implements for holding corn, the Chinese use their chop sticks for a variety of functions, including serving as "corn holders." A recent Asian visitor to our lab commented that, "The Chinese people use chop sticks for just about everything."

The current study examines the following problem: Under what conditions people are most likely to notice a second affordance for an object? A complex act, such as scooping up rice with a cup, entails grasping the cup to be used on a particular part of the cup, using a particular grip such that the cup can be wielded in such a manner as to allow rice to enter and be maintained in the cup. In effect, there is a nesting of affordances entailed in performance of a complex goal-directed action. We suggest that when the object is grasped using the same grip in order to perform both goal-directed actions, people will be more likely to recognize the second use for the object than when different grips is required for both actions.

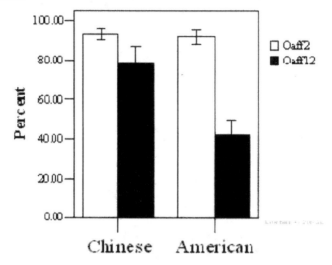

*Figure 1.* The percentage of $O_{AFF2}$ and $O_{AFF1\&2}$ identified on Task 2 by students from China and the United States.

**Method**

Twenty-eight Miami University students participated in this study. Half of the students were from China and the remainder were from the United States. There were two collections of roughly 15 objects each. The first set of objects contained objects consisting of two affordances: Some of the objects could only be used to *dig a small hole to bury a baseball in sand with*; other objects could only be used to *cut Play Doh into strips*; still other objects could be used to perform both actions ($O_{AFF1\&2}$). The second set of actions was *scooping rice from a container* and *crushing (pounding) a cracker into crumbs*. Again, objects either afforded one or both of those actions.

Before being instructed about the nature of the first action, participants were given the opportunity to pick up the various objects in front of them. Once the instructions for the first action were given, participants were then allowed to pick up each of the objects that could be used to perform that action and demonstrate how they would use it by actually performing the action (Task 1). This procedure was repeated for the second action (Task 2). After completing the second action, the experimenter asked the participant to demonstrate how $O_{AFF1\&2}$ that had not been picked up on task 2, but had been picked up on Task 1, might be used to perform the second task. These objects were treated as "missed" objects. The order in which participants performed the two actions was counterbalanced.

The actions were videotaped and digitized. Two experimenters coded the grip used for each action with the $O_{AFF1\&2}$ objects for which the first action had been identified. To code the grip, the coders used Newell et al.'s (1989) prehension taxonomy and noted the location on the object where the object was grasped when performing the required action. For the pair of actions used for a given object to be counted as "same grip," both the number of fingers and their placement on the object had to be identical. The number of *same grips* for objects that were spontaneously used to perform both actions was recorded as well as the number of different grips used when an object was not used spontaneously for the second action. This allowed us to determine the number of correct predictions (same grip when both actions were performed spontaneously and different grip when only the first action was performed spontaneously.)

## Results and Discussion

| **Chinese students**<br>*American students* | Objects (AFF1&2)<br>Used for Both Actions | Missed Objects<br>(AFF1&2) for the Second Action |
|---|---|---|
| Same Grip | **61**<br><br>*73* | **16**<br><br>*6* |
| Different Grip | **26**<br><br>*29* | **48**<br><br>*47* |

*Table 1.* For the **Chinese (bold)** and *American (italics)* students the frequency counts for spontaneously using $O_{AFF1\&2}$ for both actions and missing the $O_{AFF1\&2}$ for the second action. Each of these frequency counts is broken up into those in which the same grip was used in both actions and those in which different grips were used. The data are summed over the two pairs of actions.

Table 1 shows a summary of the frequency data for this experiment. Our hypothesis was that people would detect both affordances in objects that would be gripped the same for both actions and would fail to detect the second affordance when different grips were used. Thus, correct predictions appear in the upper left and lower right cells respectively. Overall, we correctly predicted whether an $O_{AFF1\&2}$ would be used for both actions or only for the first action for 72.2% and 77.4% of the objects for the Chinese and American students respectively. The percentages for the Chinese and American students for the dig-cut actions were 75.0% and 80.7% and for the pound-scoop actions, 67.8% and 73.6%.

We determined for each participant the proportion of correct predictions and constructed a *t-test* to ascertain whether the percentages were significantly different from chance (50%): For the Chinese students, $t$ (26 [due to camera malfunction]) = 5.95, p < .001; for the American students, $t$ (27) = 3.43, p < .002.

There are several findings of interest. First, our pilot study comparing the performance of Chinese and American students obtained a significant difference in the percentage of $O_{AFF1\&2}$ identified on Task 2, compared to the percentage of $O_{AFF2}$. That study involved only judgments of which objects supported the actions in question. The current study did not obtain a difference between the two groups of students. This may be the result of having participants actually perform the action. The task of performing the actions may have assisted participants in picking up information relevant to the action being studied. In the earlier study of perceptual judgments, the chance to explore these object properties was minimal.

Second, these results provide some support for the idea that a complex affordance, such as using an object as a tool to perform an action like scooping rice from a container and placing it into a bowl, entails detecting a nesting of affordances, each of which must be perceived and utilized in order to complete the goal-directed action. Each of the objects has to be grasped by a particular part using a particular grip so that it can be wielded appropriately to perform the intended action. Our results show that when the actor uses the same grip to perform both actions, the actor is more likely to perceive and act upon both affordances than when a different grip had to be used. But, actors did use a different grip on 29% of the cases where the same object was used to perform both tasks. This suggests that another factor is involved in detecting the second affordance of an object. In this regard we have to consider the possibility that how the object is wielded when performing the two actions may also contribute to the detection of the second affordance.

### References

Newell, K. M., Scully, D. M., Tennebaum, F., Hardiman, S. (1989). Body scale and the development of prehension. *Developmental Psychobiology, 22,* 1-14.

Ye, L., Mark, L. S. & Taliaferro, M. (June 2006). The perception of multiple affordances. Paper presented at the Spring *Meeting of the International Society for Perception and Action.* Cincinnati, Ohio.

*Acknowledgements.* This research was supported by the Committee for Faculty Research at Miami University.

*Studies in Perception & Action X*
J. B. Wagman & C. C. Pagano (Eds.)
© 2009 Taylor & Francis Group, LLC

# Changes in Anterior Deltoid Muscle Activity at the Preferred Critical Boundary for Reaching

Milena Petrovic, Adam Strang, & Leonard S. Mark

Department of Psychology, Miami University, Oxford, OH

To support a particular action mode (pattern of coordination among the limbs and torso), relevant environmental properties must be within a range determined by the action being performed and the prospective actor's body scale and biodynamic capabilities. Beyond that range the environment no longer affords the action mode and the prospective actor must engage another mode to achieve the intended goal. Research on *reaching* (Choi & Mark, 2004; Gardner et al., 2001; Mark et al., 1997) has shown that when not required to use a particular reach mode, the transition from one reach mode to another (e.g., arm-only reach to an arm-and-torso [lean] reach) occurs not at the absolute maximum distance at which an arm-only reach mode could be used, but at slightly closer distances, what Mark et al. (1997) referred to as the *preferred critical boundary*. What is responsible for the location of the preferred critical boundary?

Several studies have found that a change in the relative "comfort" of the competing action modes coincides with the location of the preferred critical boundary (Mark et al., 1997; Stasik & Mark, 2005). This raises the possibility that actors attempt to avoid awkward postures and extreme levels of muscle activity. The objective of the current study is to examine levels of muscle activity in the anterior deltoid (a superficial shoulder muscle involved in arm extension) while reaching at distances near the preferred critical boundary. We expected that muscle activity would increase as a function of distance up to the preferred critical boundary. However, when participants were not restricted on how to reach, the rate of increase was expected to change (decrease) at or near this boundary. In contrast, when they were required to use an arm-only reach, we expected the rate of increase of anterior deltoid activity to either increase or remain the same at the preferred critical boundary.

**Method**

Six men and 9 women students (age 18-34 years) participated in this study in partial fulfilment of a course requirement. Participants were seated on a height-adjustable ergonomic chair placed in front of a height-adjustable table. Table and chair height and table-to-chair distance were set relative to the body scale of each participant using the procedures followed in earlier work (e.g., Mark et al., 1997). Activity of the anterior deltoid muscle of the shoulder was measured using surface electromyography (EMG) recorded with 12-bit resolution at a bandwidth of 10-500 Hz and amplified 1000 times.

Each participant's absolute critical boundary for an arm-only reach was determined by procedures followed in earlier reach studies (Stasik & Mark, 2005), where the target object was placed at increasing distances until the participant could no longer pick up the object using an arm-only reach. The reach distances were determined from 0.65 – 1.20 of the distance of the maximum arm-only reach in increments of 0.05.

In *condition 1,* participants were instructed to reach in a manner that they found most comfortable. That is, there were no restrictions imposed on participants as to how to reach. For *condition 2* the same participants were instructed to use only an arm-only reach; this meant that reaches beyond 1.0 could not be completed. In each condition, participants reached three times at each distance in random order. The order of conditions was not counterbalanced because of our concern that performing the arm-only reaches in condition 2 might influence the measure of the preferred critical boundary.

**Results and Discussion**

For condition 1, the location of the preferred critical boundary for each participant was determined graphically by plotting the percentage of arm-only reaches as a function of distance. The preferred critical boundary was identified as the distance at which the function passed through the 50% level. The average distance of the preferred critical boundary was roughly 0.95 of the maximum arm-only reach, a finding comparable to those in previous studies. Figure 1 shows the average maximum amplitude of anterior deltoid activation as a function of reach distance. We determined the slopes of the function from 0.65-0.95 (slope = 10.6, SE = 0.96) and from 0.95 – 1.20 (slope = 2.59, SE 1.48). An ANCOVA showed that these slopes were significantly different, $F = 18.2$, (1, 147), $p < .001$, indicating that the change in reach mode modulated the rate of increase in anterior deltoid activation.

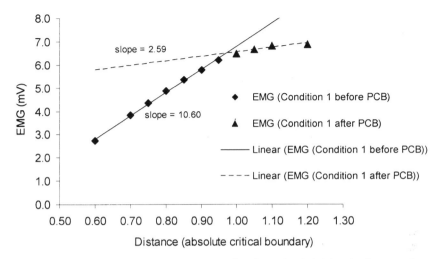

*Figure 1.* The average maximum amplitude of anterior deltoid activation as a function of reach distance is depicted by the location of the markers. The diamond and triangle markers denote reach distances closer and farther respectively than the location of the preferred critical boundary. The solid line depicts a linear regression for the distances closer than the preferred critical boundary. The broken line shows the linear regression for the distances beyond the preferred critical boundary.

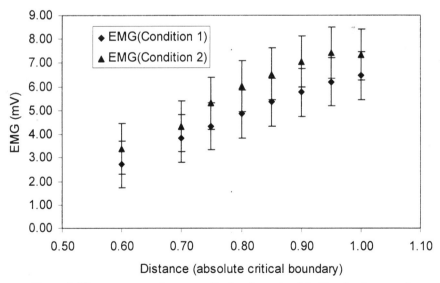

*Figure 2.* The average maximum amplitude of anterior deltoid activation as a function of reach distance is shown for conditions 1 and 2. Muscle activation was not significantly greater for condition 2 in which participants had to use an arm only reach. There was no marked change in condition 2 at the location of the preferred critical boundary.

For condition 2 in which participants used an arm only reach, the pattern of EMG activity was similar to that obtained in condition 1. Figure 2 shows that while the level of anterior deltoid activity increased up to the preferred critical boundary, the overall level of activity in condition 2 was not significantly higher than in condition 1 (free reach), $F = 0.36$, $(7,210)$, $p = 0.93$. It is possible that the restriction to reach using only an arm-only reach may have caused some additional muscle activation (tension) in condition 2.

The outcome of condition 1 suggests that actors attempted to maintain the level of anterior deltoid activation below a certain level by switching from an arm-only reach to an arm-and-torso reach (at the preferred critical boundary). However, the pattern of activation obtained in condition 2 suggests that anterior deltoid activity does not increase much beyond the level obtained at the preferred critical boundary. It may be the case that the additional reach distance (from 0.95-1.00 absolute critical boundary) does not provide sufficient opportunity for much increase in anterior deltoid activity. More likely, other muscles may have played a significant role in extending the reach capabilities. This points to the need for a future study to obtain satisfactory signals from other muscles that may be involved in reaching, such as upper trapezius, erector spinae and superspinatus. The results of this study do raise the possibility that actors attempt to maintain the level of anterior deltoid activation at a submaximal level when given the opportunity to do so. Future work must devise a more subtle method for probing these differences in muscle activation around the preferred critical boundary.

### References

Choi, H. J., & Mark, L . S. (2004). Scaling affordances for human reach actions. *Human Movement Science, 23*, 785-806.

Gardner, D. L., Mark, L. S., Ward, J. A., & Edkins, H. (2001). How do task characteristics affect the transitions between seated and standing reaches? *Ecological Psychology, 13*, 245-274.

Mark, L.S., Nemeth, K., Gardner, D.; Dainoff, M. J., Paasche, J., Duffy, M.; Grandt, K. (1997). Postural Dynamics and Preferred Critical Boundary for Visual Guided Reaching. *Journal of Experimental Psychology, 23*(5), 1365-1379.

Stasik, S., & Mark, L. S. (2005). Comfort as a determinant of the location of critical boundaries in the act of reaching. In H. Heft & K. Marsh (Eds.) *Studies in Perception and Action VII.* Mahwah, New Jersey: Erlbaum Associates. [pp 23-27]

*Studies in Perception & Action X*
J. B. Wagman & C. C. Pagano (Eds.)
© 2009 Taylor & Francis Group, LLC

# Development, Balance and Flexibility as Constraints on Perceiving Affordances

Peter B. Pufall & Kathryn Hobbs

Smith College

In previous research (Pufall & Dunbar, 1992) we extended Warren's (1984) similarity hypothesis explaining individual differences among adult humans perception of affordances to development.. That is, we hypothesized that children's perception of fit between the limits of actions of stepping onto and over obstacles scattered over their surface of action would be invariant over development because the growth rates in the upper and lower legs were constant thus fixing a skeletal invariant in the biomechanical swing of the legs for each stepping action. The optical flow of light reflectively structured surfaces in the world would be structured with respect to self by the invariant swinging structure of our gate and stepping actions.

The extended similarity hypothesis was confirmed. Six through 10-year-old children accurately perceived the critical limits of both stepping actions. The purpose of the present research is twofold. One, we are testing whether or not the developmental-similarity hypothesis can be extended developmentally to 4-year-old children. These children have the same skeletal leg proportions as older children and adults, hence there is reason to expect that they would they would accurately perceive these affordances. However, they differ dynamically from older children, and in particular in terms of static balance. Two, we are exploring whether biomechanical features affect perception. Four-year-old children cannot maintain their static balance as effectively, that is, as long, as older children. If the optic flow of information is affected by the self regulated balance of the body, then these children may not perceive a tight fit between their actions and the heights of objects within their world. In particular it may be difficult for them to perceive the critical limits of affordances. In addition, we are exploring whether or not the flexibility of hip and knee joints, joints central to stepping, are related to perception of stepping affordances.

## Method

Half of the 4-, 6-, 8- and 10-year-old children were tested in the Stepping Onto and half in the Stepping Over condition. In both conditions children identified the maximum height (MH) of a bar over or onto which they could step.

The child stood 10 feet from the testing apparatus, which consisted of a wooden bar that was moved up and down a vertical pole to which it was attached. On half of the Stepping trials the experimenter, behind an opaque screen that also hid the vertical bar, moved the bar up (Ascending trials) from well below the child's MH and on the other half she moved the bar down (Descending trials) from well above the child's MH. Each child completed 3 ascending and 3 descending trials in a randomized order. The child said "stop" at the PMH onto or over which she could step.

After the Perceived Stepping trials the children Actually Stepped onto or over an increasing number of stacked boards. The Actual Maximum Height (AMH) was the height of that stack before the child failed to successfully perform the action. Perceived Critical Limits (PCL), a measure of whether children accurately perceive the limits of their stepping functions in terms of heights of obstacles, is the average ratio of the PMH to the AMH over all six trials. A ratio of 1.00 indicates that PMH is equal to AMH, and theoretically, that children perceive precisely what the affordances of these stepping actions are.

Static balance was the number of seconds a child could stand on one leg. Flexibility of the hip joint was the angle formed by the upper leg and the vertical line of the body when the child folded one leg up into the upper body; flexibility of the knee was the angle between the upper and lower leg when the latter was bent as far as possible toward the upper leg. Greater flexibility is directly related to the degree of each bend.

## Results and Discussion

As expected, children's PMH varies directly with age $F(3,47) = 44.22$, $p < .000$), that is, with increasing age children's PMH is significantly higher than it was the year before ($p < 005$). In contrast to the prediction from our *similarity model* PCL varied with age ($F(3,47) = 6.95$, $p < .001$); post hoc analyses indicate the age effect is reflected only in the differences between the youngest children's estimates and those of the three age older groups ($p < .007$). The latter finding replicates our previous work, while the former indicates that the model cannot be generalized to children younger than age 6 years. More precisely, because the proportional relation of leg to lower leg is an invariant across the full age range tested it appears that the geometric constraint set by children's skeletal structures is not sufficient for them to perceive accurately the critical limits of stepping affordances. Children at all ages overestimate the height of obstacles they can step onto more than they overestimate the height they can step over ($F(3,47) = 6.95$, $p < .001$). In the absence of a significant interaction between age and stepping actions, it appears that the extent of this difference persists over development.

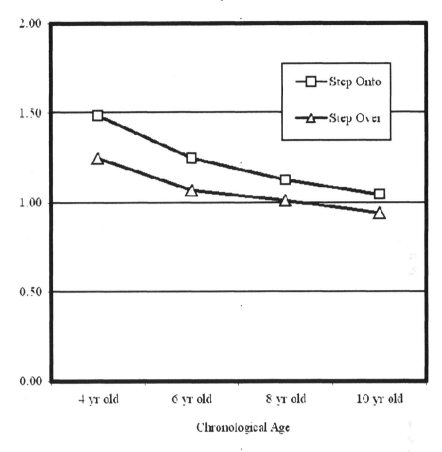

*Figure 1:* Mean Perceived Critical Limits expressed as the ratio of children's PMH to the AMH of obstacles onto or over which they can step.

Children at all ages perceived a higher MH on trials when the bar was descending than when it was ascending ($F(1,48) = 78.44$, $p < .000$). When this difference is represented by DPCL and APCL, it is clear that children's overestimations of the CLs is due primarily to their judgments on the descending trials (Figure 1). The fact that children perform so well on the ascending trials yet overestimate on the descending trials over development and across stepping functions raises the possibility that descending trials generate error linked to our method. To be sure, asking children to perceive a critical limit with respect to a moving an object challenges the ecological validity of the psychophysical method we used, however, the fact that they accurately perceive their limits on one kind of trial and not another suggests that our method should be examined not because of movement but the direction of movement. On ascending trials the bar is first situated with respect to the surface of locomotion and affords both stepping actions. By contrast on the descending trials children may not initially perceive it with respect to the surface locomotion and it is beyond the limits of the actions by which we are asking children to scale their physical world. That is, the descending trial is less ecological than the ascending trial.

Even if this aspect of our method is a contaminant, it does not account for the fact that the four-year-old children do not perceive what their world affords as precisely as older children do even on the ascending trials. We hypothesized that children may vary in the accuracy with which they perceive stepping affordances because of constraints on their skeletal structure. Children did not vary over development with respect to hip or joint flexibility, but they differ significantly with respect to static balance ($F(3,52) = 8.72$, $p < .000$). The youngest children's static balance time was significantly less than the static balance of the other three age groups ($p < .005$). That is, the abrupt development between 4 and 6 years of age in children's perception of CLs is mirrored in their development of static balance. Moreover, correlations between age and balance ($r = -.52$, $p < .000$) are significantly correlated. The negative correlation indicates that the longer children maintained their static balance the more accurately they perceived the fit between stepping actions and whether or not the height of objects are within the limits of affording those actions.

In sum, these findings suggest that the *similarity model* needs developmental fine-tuning. Although young children share the same skeletal proportions of leg length to upper and lower leg detecting this invariant relation the geometry of the leg and actions within the world is built from moving through the world and detecting the flow of visual information specific to forms of action. The fidelity of this information appears to depend on static balance, at least, and perhaps dynamic balance. Static balance may have both a developmental role as well as account for individual differences in older children's perception of affordances.

## References

Pufall, P. B., & Dunbar, C. (1992). Perceiving whether or not the world affords stepping onto and over: A developmental study. *Ecological Psychology*, *4*(1), 17-38.

Warren, W. H. (1984). Perceiving affordances: Visual guidance of stair climbing. *Journal of Experimental Psychology: Human Perception and Performance*, *10*, 683-703.

*Studies in Perception & Action X*
J. B. Wagman & C. C. Pagano (Eds.)
© 2009 Taylor & Francis Group, LLC

# Ecometrics of Step-Over Height

Masaki Ueno, Shogo Hirata, Hideyuki Okuzumi,
& Mitsuru Kokubun

Tokyo Gakugei University

Ecometrics is one of the central themes of ecological psychology (Warren, 1984). In this study, we investigate the choice of actions when walking through an obstacle, that is, when adults choose stepping-over or passing-under a rope, focusing on the relationship between choice and the subject's height. In addition, we also measure school-age children to investigate the developmental trends of ecometrics.

**Method**

The subjects were 41 adults (23 males and 18 females) and 14 children aged 10 years (7 males, 7 females). Adults ranged from 19 to 30 years of age (22.29 ± 2.18 years); the height of the males ranged from 160 to 183 cm (170.13 ± 5.22 cm), while the females ranged from 148 to 165 cm (157.50 ± 5.12 cm). The height of the male children ranged from 128 to 147 cm (135.29 ± 6.97 cm); the female children ranged from 130 to 146 cm (137.57 ± 6.48 cm).

We devised an apparatus that could draw a rope tight, and allowed the rope height to be adjusted between 20 cm to 130 cm from the floor. Subjects stood 2 m in front of the rope, and were asked to walk beyond the rope by stepping-over or passing under it. The rope height was changed up and down in 5 cm increments from the subject's waist, and presented at random. At each rope height, we recorded whether subjects stepped over or passed under, and whether they hit the rope while doing so.

We define the height of the highest stepping-over rope as the "transition point." That is to say, subjects pass under the rope that is higher than the transition point. In this study, to analyze the relationship between the transition point and the subject's height, we calculate a "transition ratio" by dividing the transition point by the subject's height. We use the transition point and transition ratio for the analysis.

*Ueno, Hirata, Okuzumi, & Kokubun*

**Results and Discussion**

Table 1 shows the means and standard deviations of the transition point and transition ratio in both age groups for both sexes. The transition point for adults was obviously higher than that for 10-year-olds. In addition, while the transition point in adult males is higher than that of females, the difference by sex was not obvious in children. Transition point was analyzed by a two-way (age × sex) ANOVA, which demonstrated a significant effect of age ($F_{1, 51}$ = 73.64, $p < .05$), no significant effect of sex ($F_{1, 51}$ = 2.63, $p > .05$), but a significant interaction ($F_{1, 51}$ = 7.09, $p < .05$). A simple main effect test demonstrated a significant effect at the 5% level for a sex difference only in adults. These results show that the development of task performance in this study is a process in which the transition point rises with age, and the difference by sex emerges as males and females begin to differ in height. Interestingly, the transition ratio in each age group was almost the same regardless of sex. That is, all values are 0.4x. The transition ratio was analyzed by a two-way (age × sex) ANOVA, which showed no significant effects of age ($F_{1, 51}$ = 2.89, $p > .05$), sex ($F_{1, 51}$ = 0.06, $p > .05$), nor their interaction ($F_{1, 51}$ = 0.64, $p > .05$). Therefore, the transition ratio is almost the same in each group.

Table 1. Mean and standard deviation of transition point and transition ratio

|  |  | transition point | | transition ratio | |
| --- | --- | --- | --- | --- | --- |
|  |  | M | SD | M | SD |
| Adults | males | 75.22 | 4.73 | 0.44 | 0.03 |
|  | females | 68.17 | 5.67 | 0.43 | 0.03 |
| Children aged 10 years | males | 56.71 | 5.47 | 0.42 | 0.03 |
|  | females | 58.43 | 6.02 | 0.42 | 0.03 |

These results suggest that although the rope-height transition actually occurred at different points in adults and 10-year-olds, the transition standard is the same. If we describe the relationship between the transition point and subject's height in the adults, the defining expression is as follows:

$$TP / H = 0.44 \ (SD = .03) \ \text{[TP: transition point, H: subject's height]}.$$

That is, adults transition at a rope height that is 0.44 times their own height. The transition ratio value for 10-year-olds was the same as for adults. These findings show a robust law of ecometrics in performing the task regardless of age. Mishima (1994) reported an expression of the transition of stepping-over and passing-under based on leg length that indicated the same tendency as ours. Whereas his study used a cognitive task to evaluate stepping-over and passing-under, our study used a motor task. Note that since our study used a motor task, a few subjects touched the rope accidentally in each age group. Subjects who touched the rope accidentally, in effect, failed to accomplish the task safely. It remains to be seen whether analysis of the relationship between the transition and its safety can be refined. In addition, evaluating a wider age range of children would allow us to analyze the developmental process of task performance.

### References

Mishima, H. (1994). Perceiving affordances for switching two actions, 'stepping-over' and 'passing-under'. *Japanese Journal of Psychology*. 64(6). 469-475. (In Japanese with English abstract.)

Warren, W. H. (1984). Perceiving affordances: Visual guidance of stair climbing. *Journal of Experimental Psychology: Human Perception and Performance*.10.683-703.

*Acknowledgements.* The authors would like to thank the participants who made this work possible.

*Studies in Perception & Action X*
J. B. Wagman & C. C. Pagano (Eds.)
© 2009 Taylor & Francis Group, LLC

# Investigating the Information Used To Detect An Affordance For Maximum Distance Throws

## Qin Zhu[1] & Geoffrey Bingham[2]

[1]Division of Kinesiology and Health, University of Wyoming, Laramie, USA
[2]Department of Psychological and Brain Sciences, Indiana University, Bloomington, USA

Previous studies (Bingham et al., 1989; Zhu & Bingham, 2008) have shown that people with sufficient throwing experience were able to heft and select the optimal weight for different sized graspable objects to be thrown to a maximum distance using their skilled throwing arm. The selected objects were indeed thrown to the farthest distances, indicating that throwing affordances of the objects were well perceived. However, it remains unclear what information is made available by hefting and used to detect throwing affordance.

According to the ecological approach to perception and action (Gibson, 1986), information is required to both detect the useful structure of the environment and assemble actions used to manipulate the environment. This assertion leads to the smart perceptual mechanism hypothesis (Runeson, 1977), in light of which, hefting acts as a smart perceptual device to detect information about optimal objects for throwing (Bingham et al., 1989). Given hefting and throwing are both actions performed with the thrown objects, the objects must affect the dynamics of both actions. Bingham et al. hypothesized that object size and weight both affected the dynamics of hefting (size was found to affect the stiffness at the wrist, and optimal weight was assumed to control resulting frequency of movement), and were likewise presumed to affect the dynamics of long distance throwing. However, recent studies showed that object size and weight did not equally affect the dynamics of throwing (Zhu & Bingham, 2008). Object weight was the only variable to affect throwing (by constraining the release velocity), while object size only played role in projectile motion (after the object has left the hand) to affect the throwing distance. This finding invited further investigation on the information underlying the perception of throwing affordance.

## Experiment 1

We began our investigation by asking whether the information is intrinsic or acquired. Considering that maximum distance throwing is a skill that has to be learned, the perception of throwing affordances would presumably also be learned, but if so, how? Perceivers could learn a single valued function (throwing distance) of two variables (object size and weight) through function learning (Busemeyer et al., 1993), or they could learn to direct their attention to the relevant information that reflects the inherent relationship between the environment (object size and weight) and the result of action used to manipulate that environment (throwing distance), as predicted by the smart perceptual mechanism. These two approaches can be distinguished using their respective requirements for adequate sampling of the space. The former requires sampling of the entire space, but the latter does not.

### Method

Forty-eight spherical objects were made with eight weights in each of six sizes. The matrix of object size and weight was constructed so that three subsets of objects could be created: a set of six objects of a constant weight, a set of six objects of a constant density, and a set of six objects of a constant size. One object was shared by all three subsets. Twenty-four unskilled adult throwers were initially asked to heft all 48 objects and judge the optimal weight for throwing in each size. Next, they actually threw every object in an outdoor field without seeing the resulting distances of throws. Then, they started a month of throwing practice, during which they were divided into 4 groups so that 3 groups practiced throwing with vision using one of three sets of objects (constant size, constant weight or constant density). The fourth group used objects of constant density without vision. After the month of practice, hefting judgments, throwing (with vision) and then hefting judgments again were tested with the full set of objects.

### Results and Discussion

As shown in Figure 1, the preferred objects corresponded to those being thrown to the farthest after practice, and this can only be seen in vision groups independently of the practice set ($F_{1, 15} = 41.98$, $p < 0.001$), indicating that perceptual information was discovered during learning to throw, and it was achieved through a smart perceptual mechanism. The facts that the no-vision group did not acquire the affordance perception and that all judgments became better after seeing throws suggested that visual feedback is required for acquiring the information about the affordance for throwing.

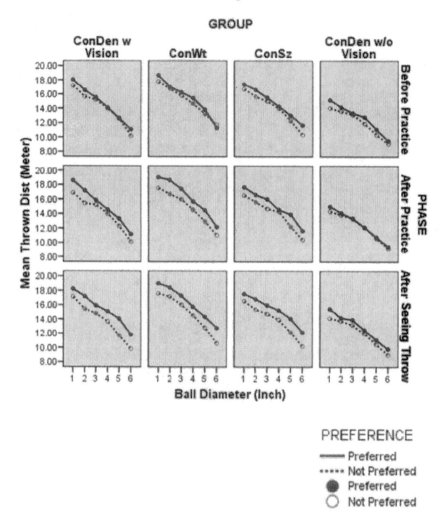

*Figure 1* Mean throwing distances achieved by unskilled throwers after practice (separated for each group) as a function of size and preference across the hefting judgment phases. Filled circles connected with a solid line represent the preferred objects. Unfilled circles connected with a dashed line represent the un-preferred objects.

## Experiment 2

We next addressed what serves as the information for the affordance for throwing? Previous studies have consistently shown that the optimal weights selected for throwing co-varied with object sizes in a function corresponding to that of the classic size-weight illusion, in which objects of increasing size must weigh more to be perceived of equal heaviness. It is possible that preferred weights at each different size are perceived as equally heavy.

**Method**

The same objects were used. Twelve skilled adult throwers were recruited to perform two hefting judgment tests. They were first asked to select optimal objects at each size for maximum distance throws, and then they were asked to select objects at each size that were felt equally heavy to a comparison object. Two sizes of comparison objects were used (1-inch and 6-inch). Participants were randomly divided into two groups to perform the judgments. In each group, the comparison object used was actually the one selected by the same participant before as optimal for throwing, but this was not known by the participant.

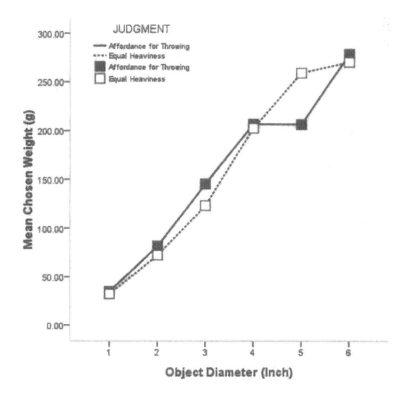

*Figure 2* Mean chosen weights from both comparison groups as a function of object diameter and judgment task. Filled squares connected with a solid line represent the judgments of optimal weights for throwing; unfilled squares connected with a dashed line represent the judgments of objects that were felt equally heavy to the given comparison object.

**Results and Discussion**

As shown in Figure 2, there was no significant difference between two judgments in both groups, indicating that the objects selected to be optimal for throwing were also felt equally heavy to all throwers. Chosen weights increased as object became larger, suggesting that both judgments were subject to the size-weight illusion.

**Conclusion**

The information about the affordance for maximum distance throws is distinguished through learning to throw. It is based on the perceived heaviness. People learn to detect the heaviness that is optimal for long distance throws. Vision was required to allow the perceiver to identify the optimal value of heaviness for throwing. Once the optimal heaviness is identified, the affordance can be perceived, and the perception of the affordance can be generalized to any situation where the optimal heaviness can be detected.

**References**

Bingham, G., Schmidt, R., & Rosenblum, L. (1989). Hefting for a maximum distance throw: A smart perceptual mechanism. *Journal of Experimental Psychology: Human Perception and Performance*, 15 (3), 507-528.

Busemeyer, J. R., & Townsend, J. T. (1993). Decision Field Theory: A dynamic cognitive approach to decision making. *Psychological Review*, 100, 432-459.

Gibson, J. J. (1986). The ecological approach to visual perception. Hillsdale, NJ: Lawrence Erlbaum Associates.

Runeson, S. (1977). On the possibility of "smart" perceptual mechanisms. *Scandinavia Journal of Psychology*, 18, 172-179.

Zhu, Q., & Bingham, G.P. (2008). Is hefting to perceive the affordance for throwing a smart perceptual mechanism? *Journal of Experimental Psychology: Human Perception and Performance*, 34 (4), 929-943.

*Studies in Perception & Action X*
J. B. Wagman & C. C. Pagano (Eds.)
© 2009 Taylor & Francis Group, LLC

# Chapter 5:

# Posture

*Studies in Perception & Action X*
J. B. Wagman & C. C. Pagano (Eds.)
© 2009 Taylor & Francis Group, LLC

# A Closed-Loop Controller
# to model Postural Coordination

V. Bonnet[1], B. Bardy[2], P. Fraisse[1],
N. Ramdani[1], J. Lagarde[2], & S. Ramdani[2]

[1]LIRMM UMR 5506 CNRS Univ. Montpellier II (France)
[2] EDM EA 2991, University Montpellier I (France)

Within the framework of coordination dynamics (Kelso, 1995), Bardy and collaborators (e.g., Bardy et al., 1999) analyzed the whole body joint coordination in the sagittal plane during a visual tracking task. They proposed a collective variable capturing in a simple way the complex interactions operating within the postural system: the *relative phase* between the ankles and the hips. Two coordination modes were observed depending on target frequency: An *in-phase* mode for low frequencies and an *anti-phase* mode for high frequencies. Furthermore, this postural task allowed the observation of several self-organized properties, such as phase transition, multi-stability, critical fluctuations and hysteresis.

In a recent attempt to implement in artificial agents the natural coordination modes observed in humans (Bonnet et al., 2007) we examined in more details the coordination modes obtained by Bardy et al. and implemented them in HOAP-3 and HRP2 humanoid robots. We were able to demonstrate that the in-phase mode corresponds to the *minimum energy mode* for low frequencies and that the anti-phase mode is the only mode able to *maintain balance* for high frequencies.

However, the approach described above considers only steady state behaviours and thus is not capable of capturing the transient dynamics observed during human postural tracking. The goal of the current study is to propose a non-linear closed-loop model of the supra-postural behaviour documented by Bardy, composed of a double inverted pendulum (DIP) as biomechanical model, a controller in operational space, a dynamical (time-varying) torque saturation to ensure balance and passive spring-damping systems to simulate human joint stiffness. The ability for the model to reproduce the observed biological couplings should ameliorate or simplify balance control in humanoids.

## Method

The task realized to collect human data is similar to the one used by Bardy et al. (1999) and involved standing participants to track a moving target with their head. The experiment was performed with 11 healthy male subjects, with mean age 25, mean weight of 75kg and mean size of 1.79 m. Participants were asked to stand on a force plate in front of a real target moved by a linear motor in the antero-posterior direction, with the knees locked and the soles in permanent contact with the ground. The motion of the target was sinusoidal (amplitude of 10 cm), the frequency increased from 0.1 Hz to 0.65 Hz by 0.05 Hz steps and during 10 periods. To capture the joint positions, a motion VICON TM capture system was used, with 8 cameras tracking 15 makers on the right side of the body.

## Modeling the tracking task

The focus of the Bardy et al. (1999) study was on hip and ankle joints. For this reason, a DIP in the sagittal plane was used as a biomechanical model. The human joint properties were also considered by adding passive spring-damping systems at each joint of the rigid DIP. To complete the model, the issue of maintaining the center of pressure (CoP) inside the base of support (BoS) needed to be addressed. In the human motor control literature, there are no obvious evidences that CoP location is directly controlled by the central nervous system (CNS). In addition Bonnet et al. (2007) emphasized the fact that the postural system changes its coordination mode when the CoP reaches the BoS limit. Finally, since CoP location is a function of the ankle torque, we proposed to use an adaptive ankle torque saturation, function of the dynamic variables. Thus, the CoP location was not controlled *per se* but just bounded.

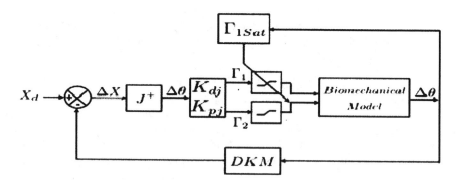

*Figure 1.* Block diagram of the postural coordination controller.

All these components were integrated in the close loop controller depicted in Fugure 1, with $J^+$ the Jacobian pseudo-inverse matrix, *DKM* the direct kinematic model and *Kp-Kd* the proportional-derivative gains of the head tracking regulator.

## Results and Discussion

In this section, human experimental data are compared with the close-loop simulations results. The evolution of the controller reference is the same as the head position given in the experiment. Figures 2 and 3 presents typical human data and simulations for one subject of about 1.8 m in height and 75 kg in weight.

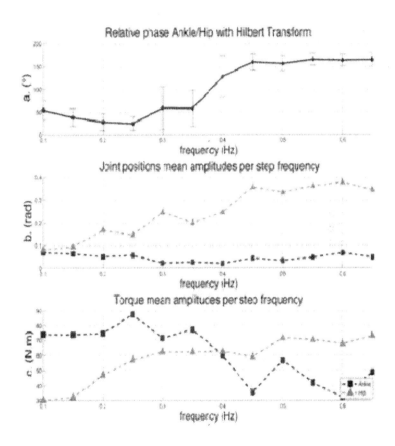

*Figure 2.* Typical experimental data. (a) Ankle/hip relative phase showing a transition; (b) Peak-to-peak joint position. Hip position is larger than ankle position for anti-phase, and conversely for in-phase; (c) Joint torque amplitude.

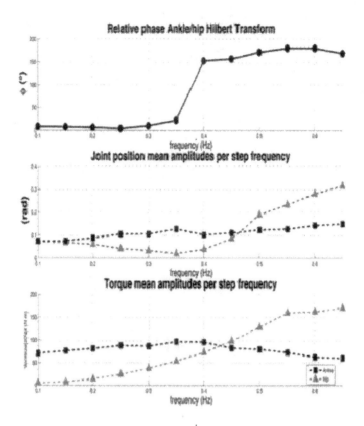

*Figure 3.* Typical simulation data. (a) Ankle/hip relative phase showing a transition; (b) Peak-to-peak joint position. Hip position is larger than ankle position for anti-phase, and conversely for in-phase; (c) Joint torque amplitude.

The closed-loop controller model developed is able to reproduce non-linear human postural phenomena such as phase transition, joint position, torques, or hysteresis (Figure 4). The closed-loop modelling approach offers a better under-standing of postural coordination dynamics. The knowledge of the full biome-chanical parameters permits to determine the mechanical impact in the joint coordination mode.

Two factors appears to contribute to the phase transition in our model:

 - *Energy:* The controller uses a pseudo-inverse matrix, and hence this closed-loop system minimizes by construction an energetic criterion.

 - *Balance:* The ankle torque saturates when frequency increases, and this saturation contributes to the shift from in phase to antiphase in which the postural system acts mainly on the hip torque.

In conclusion, it appears that our model of postural coordination is able to capture behavioral invariants repeatedly observed during human postural tracking. In addition, some differences still observed between experimental and simulated results could be reduced by using of a more complete muscle model, using of a joint-varying active stiffness.

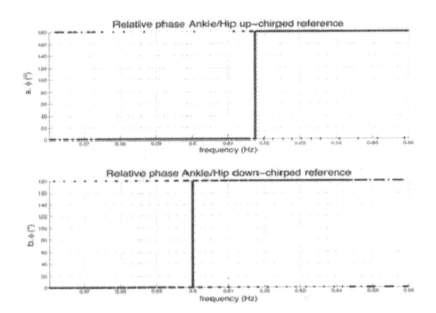

*Figure 4.* A typical simulation of hysteresis. (a) The relative phase for up-chirped reference signal. (b) The relative phase for down-chirped signal.

### References

Bardy, B. G., Marin, L., Stoffregen, T. A., & Bootsma, R. J. (1999). Postural coordination modes considered as emergent phenomena. *Journal of Experimental Psychology: Human Perception and Performance, 25,* 1284-1301.

Bonnet, V., Fraisse, P., Lagarde, J., Ramdani, N., Ramdani, S. & Bardy, B. G. (2007). Modelling of the human postural coordination to improve the humanoid control of balance. *IEE Int. Conf. on Humanoid Robots.*

Bonnet, V., Fraisse, P., Lagarde, J., Ramdani, N., Ramdani, S. & Bardy, B. G. (2008). Modelling postural coordination dynamics using a closed-loop controller. *IEE Int. Conf. on Humanoid Robots,* 61-66.

Kelso, J (1995). *Dynamics patterns the self-organization of brain and behavior.* The MIT Press.

*Studies in Perception & Action X*
J. B. Wagman & C. C. Pagano (Eds.)
© 2009 Taylor & Francis Group, LLC

# Postural Stabilization of Visual Performance at Sea

## Fu-Chen Chen[1], Yawen Yu[1], Sebastien Villard[2], & Thomas A. Stoffregen[1]

[1]University of Minnesota, [2]University of Montpellier-1, France

Classically, theory and research relating to the control of stance have focused on the avoidance of falling, that is, maintaining the body's center of mass over the base of support. Postural control certainly helps to avoid falling, but it may have other functions, as well. Postural actions move the center of mass, but they also alter the position and motion of the head and, consequently, of the eyes. Postural stabilization of vision has been demonstrated in a variety of contexts; children (Jordan et al., 2008) and the elderly (Prado et al., 2007), eye movements (Stoffregen et al., 2007) and fixation (Stoffregen et al., 1999), reading (Stoffregen et al., 2000) and so on. In most previous cases have involved unperturbed stance, such that postural motion arose entirely from the person. In some cases, standing participants have been exposed to optical motion, as for example a moving room (Stoffregen et al. 2006). In this study, we examined postural stabilization of vision in a situation involving motion of the surface of support.

We studied experienced maritime crewmembers on a ship at sea. Relations between body motion and the performance of visual tasks are of increasing importance in naval applications, as work becomes increasingly focused on computer interaction. While at sea, standing participants performed visual tasks. We varied the degree of ocular stability required for visual performance. Following Stoffregen et al. (2000), we predicted that sway would be reduced during performance of a visually demanding task, relative to stance during performance of a task having reduced visual demand. We also varied stance width, that is, the distance between the feet during stance. Wider stance is associated with reductions in the magnitude of spontaneous postural sway (e.g., Day et al., 1993), but this relationship has not been evaluated in the context of continuous motion of the support surface (cf. Henry et al., 2001). We predicted that the magnitude of sway would be negatively related to stance width. Previous studies of standing sway in moving environments have been limited to ship simulators, and have not manipulated stance width or visual task demand (e.g., Dobie et al., 2003; Nawayseh & Griffin, 2006).

**Method**

The study was conducted aboard the R/V Atlantis, on the 5$^{th}$ day of a 6-day cruise from San Diego to Mazatlan, Mexico. The Atlantis was 84 m long and displaced 3500 tons, and cruised at 12 knots. Ten crewmembers participated on a volunteer basis. Crew ranged in age from 25 to 54 years, and had from 1 to 28 years experience working at sea.

Postural data were collected using a force plate (AMTI, Watertown, MA) sampled at 40 Hz. Visual tasks and targets were the same as those used by Stoffregen et al. (2000).

The study was conducted in the ship's Main Laboratory, a large room located amidships on the main deck. The force plate was positioned near a wall, and visual targets were affixed to the wall with Velcro. Targets were adjusted to be at eye height for each participant. The visual targets consisted of sheets of white paper 13.5 cm x 17 cm and mounted on rigid cardboard. For the Inspection task, the paper was blank. For the Search task, the sheet was printed with English text in a 12 point sans serif font. When on the force plate, participants were facing athwartship (rather than fore and aft), such that roll motion of the ship would be corrected by sway in the body's AP axis, and pitch motion of the ship would be corrected by sway in the body's ML axis.

Participants stood on the force plate with their heels on a line that was 1.0 m from the visual target. Lateral foot placement was determined by three pairs of lines on the plate, such that the heels were 5 cm, 17 cm or 30 cm apart and the angle between the feet was 10°. In the Inspection task, the target consisted of a blank sheet of white paper; participants were instructed to keep their gaze within the borders of the target. In the Search task the target was one of 4 blocks of text, each consisting of 13 or 14 lines of text. Prior to each trial the participant was given a target letter (A, R, N, or S), and asked to count the number of times the target letter appeared in the block of text. At the end of each Search trial, the participant reported the number of letters counted, and their position in the text at the end of the trial. During testing, the sea state was 2 on the Beaufort scale (Beer, 1997).

We used a 2 × 3 design with one trial per participant in each of six conditions. Each trial was 65 s long. We assessed postural activity in terms of the positional variability of the center of pressure (COP).

**Results and Discussion**

The results are summarized in Figure 1. Analysis of variance revealed a significant main effect of stance width, $F_{(2,8)} = 33.64$, $p < .001$, for movement in the body's ML axis (Figure 1A). This effect is similar to land-based demonstrations of an inverse relation between stance width and the magnitude of ML sway (e.g., Day et al., 1993). We also found a main effect of visual task, $F_{(1,9)} = 12.35$, $p = .007$, for movement in the body's AP axis (Figure 1B). When performing the Search task, the magnitude of sway was reduced, related to sway during the Inspection task. This effect replicates a finding of Stoffregen et al. (2000). None of the participants reported seasickness at any point during the cruise.

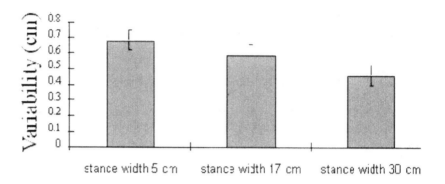

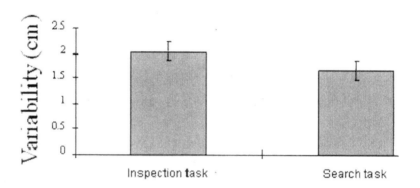

*Figure 1.* Mean positional variability of the COP. Body's ML axis (Top). Body's AP axis (Bottom).

We replicated the classical finding that the magnitude of postural sway is inversely related to the distance between the feet in side-by-side stance (e.g., Day et al., 1993), and we showed that this effect occurs on a ship at sea. This finding suggests that variation in stance width might be used by sailors, on a task-specific basis, to control the magnitude of sway at sea. Appropriate varia-tions in stance width would be related to the nature of the visual task at hand, to the sea state (i.e., wave height), and to the ship's heading relative to the wind. Complex and highly variable relations between these factors suggest that learn-ing could be slow, which is compatible with anecdotal reports that it often takes several days to get one's "sea legs".

We also replicated the finding of Stoffregen et al. (2000) that the magnitude of sway was reduced during a reading-like task, relative to sway during a less demanding visual task, and we extended this finding to nautical conditions. In our study, experienced sailors modulated their stance in ways that would tend to maximize both visual performance and the efficiency of postural control. Future research should examine how this skill is acquired, and whether the relation between sway and visual performance actually is functional.

### References

Beer, T. (1997). *Environmental oceanography*. Boca Raton, FL: CRC Press.

Day, B.L., Steiger, M.J., Thompson, P.D., & Marsen, C.D. (1993). Effects of vision and stance width on human body motion when standing: implications for afferent control of lateral sway. *Journal of Physiology, 469*, 479–499.

Dobie, T. G., May, J. G., & Flanagan, M. (2003). The influence of visual reference on stance and walking on a moving surface. *Aviation, Space, and Environmental Medicine, 74*, 838-845.

Henry, S. M., Fung, J., & Horak, F. B. (2001). Effect of stance width on multidirectional postural responses. *Journal of Physiology, 85*, 559-570.

Jordan, A., Wade, M. G., & Yoshida, K. (2008, June). Postural support for visual performance in children at risk for developmental coordination disorder. Talk given at NASPSPA 2008, Niagara Falls, Canada.

Nawayseh, N., & Griffin, M. J. (2006). Effect of frequency, magnitude and direction of translational and rotational oscillation on the postural stability of standing people. *Journal of Sound and Vibration, 298*, 725–754.

Prado, J. M., Stoffregen, T. A., & Duarte, M. (2007). Postural sway during dual tasks in young and elderly adults. *Gerontology, 53*, 274-281.

Stoffregen, T. A., Bardy, B. G., Bonnet, C. T., Hove, P., & Oullier, O. (2007). Postural sway and the frequency of horizontal eye movements. *Motor Control, 11*, 86-102.

Stoffregen, T. A., Hove, P., Schmit, J., & Bardy, B. G. (2006). Voluntary and involuntary postural responses to imposed optic flow. *Motor Control, 10*, 24-33.

Stoffregen, T. A., Pagulayan, R. J., Bardy, B. G., & Hettinger, L. J. (2000). Modulating postural control to facilitate visual performance. *Human Movement Science, 19*, 203-220.

Stoffregen, T. A., Smart, L. J., Bardy, B. G., & Pagulayan, R. J. (1999). Postural stabilization of looking. *Journal of Experimental Psychology: Human Perception & Performance, 25*, 1641-1658.

*Acknowledgements*. We thank Captain A. D. Colburn and Liz Caporelli of the Woods Hole Oceanographic Institution, who made this study possible.

*Studies in Perception & Action X*
J. B. Wagman & C. C. Pagano (Eds.)
© 2009 Taylor & Francis Group, LLC

# Immediate Awareness of the Surrounding Environment in the Form of Optical Pushes

Makoto Inagami & Ryuzo Ohno

Department of Built Environment, Tokyo Institute of Technology, Japan

Gordon Cullen (1971), a keen urban designer, described the experience of walking through townscapes as "a journey through pressures and vacuums, a sequence of exposures and enclosures" (p.10). During daily locomotion, humans are constantly aware of the environment that surrounds their bodies. They immediately feel the presence of surrounding surfaces, rather than intellectually understand the geometrical layout. This article deals with such immediate environmental awareness, which was aptly described as "pressure" by Cullen.

We have thus far attempted to investigate environmental awareness by an original method (e.g., Inagami & Ohno, 2008; Inagami, Ohno, & Tsujiuchi, 2008). Our method uses the "feeling of pressure" ("appaku-kan" in Japanese) caused by the surrounding environment. It is defined as a feeling that changes in accordance with the extent to which the point of observation is spatially enclosed. The feeling is similar to what has been studied as subjective enclosure or closeness in environmental psychology (e.g., Stamps & Smith, 2002). In our experiments, participants continuously rate their feelings while walking through a daily environment. Our method analyzes the relationship between the participants' ratings and several environmental measurements (e.g., visible area of buildings) to capture their awareness of the surroundings.

This article analyzes the data obtained in the experiment reported by Inagami et al. (2008) through another method. On the basis of the result, we discuss the relationship between environmental awareness and a phenomenon called "optical push" (e.g., Shaw & Kinsella-Shaw, 2007).

## Method

The experiment was conducted using a 425-meter outdoor route in our university campus. As shown in Figure 1, the route contained various characteristic places such as a tunnel, a hill, and areas surrounded by tall buildings. Fourteen graduate students (seven males and seven females) individually participated in the experiment. They continuously rated their feelings of pressure while walking along the route. Their ratings were outputted by turning a dial on a portable rating device. Since the data were recorded in time series, we converted them to 850 pieces of data in such a way that each piece approximately corresponded to 850 points at 0.5-meter intervals along the route. In addition, the converted data were standardized for every participant and then averaged across all participants.

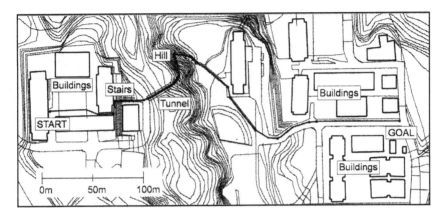

*Figure 1.* Experimental route in our university campus.

To measure the changes in the environmental layout along the route, we used our original computer program (for details see Ohno, 1991). The measurement was based on the environmental data (site plan, land configuration, and tree data) created with computer-aided design (CAD) software. We set 850 points of observation at 0.5-meter intervals along the route, which were at the level of 1.5 meters above the ground. At every point, the program radiated 1944 scanning lines all around (72 horizontally × 27 vertically) and recorded the distances to the surrounding environmental surfaces. The measurement was limited to within a 72-meter radius of each observing point.

As a variable to describe the environmental layout, we adopted the averages of the measured distances. According to ecological optics (Gibson, 1979), environmental information is conveyed by the global flow of the ambient optic array. The optic flow radially expands from the direction of locomotion and contracts toward the opposite direction. The flow velocity of each environmental component not only varies with the angular deviation from the focus of expansion, but is also inversely proportional to the distance from the observing point. In view of the optical properties, we divided the surrounding environment into three parts with respect to the angular deviation (front [0–60°], middle [60–120°], and back [120–180°]) and calculated the average distances to the environmental surfaces for each part.

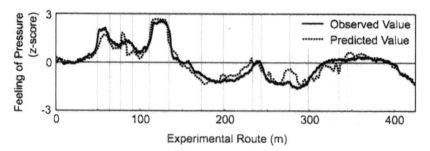

*Figure 2.* Prediction of the feeling of pressure along the route. The observed values are the mean ratings for all participants ($N = 14$).

## Results and Discussion

To analyze the relationship between the participants' ratings and environmental variables, we performed a multiple regression analysis using the following model:

$$Fp = \beta_0 - \beta_1 D_f - \beta_2 D_m - \beta_3 D_b, \qquad (1)$$

where $Fp$ is the feeling of pressure and $D_f$, $D_m$, and $D_b$ are the average distances to the front, middle, and back parts of the surrounding environment, respectively. The parameters $\beta_0$, $\beta_1$, $\beta_2$, and $\beta_3$ were estimated to be 3.097, .085, .002, and .048, respectively ($p < .01$ in all cases). Figure 2 illustrates the variations in the observed (i.e., rated) and predicted values along the route. The resultant coefficient of determination is .88, indicating that the participants' ratings have a high correlation with the variables of the environmental layout.

This result suggests that the participants continuously felt pressure from the surrounding environment while proceeding along the route. Their ratings are considered as the integration of the pressures caused by each of the surrounding surfaces. During the rating task, the constantly changing feeling was outputted directly by the rating device. The rating was conducted intuitively without the intervention of any intellectual process such as the estimation of the size of the surrounding surfaces. Viewed in this light, the feeling of pressure is environmental awareness itself rather than something that derives from it. In other words, humans are immediately aware of the surrounding environment in the form of the feeling of pressure caused by the surfaces.

We speculate that the feeling of pressure could be interpreted as the so-called "optical push." As an example of the phenomenon, Shaw and Kinsella-Shaw (2007) cited an error that pilots sometimes make while controlling low flying airplanes. Even if the pilots intend to keep a fixed altitude, they involuntarily change the altitude when crossing the boundary between sea and land. The abrupt change in the density of texture induces a virtual force. The pilots generate an action as if being pushed by the optical flow. In our view, even during daily locomotion such as in our experiment, the same sort of force potentially acts on the perceivers. They are pushed by the global flow of the ambient optic array and thereby continuously feel varying degree of pressure toward the environment surrounding their bodies. The pressure moderately guides, rather than forcibly controls, their locomotion through the environment. Given this perspective, environmental awareness could be conceptualized not as mental representation but as interaction with the surrounding surfaces.

## References

Cullen, G. (1971). *The concise townscape.* London: Architectural Press.

Gibson, J. J. (1979). *The ecological approach to visual perception.* Boston: Houghton Mifflin Company.

Inagami, M. & Ohno, R. (2008). Anisotropy of environmental awareness caused by spatial changes during locomotion. In C. Hölscher (Ed.), *Spatial Cognition 2008: Poster Presentations* (pp.97–100). Bremen/Freiburg: SFB/TR 8 Spatial Cognition.

Inagami, M., Ohno, R., & Tsujiuchi, R. (2008). Phenomenal awareness of the surrounding space: An ecological perspective. *Cognitive Studies: Bulletin of the Japanese Cognitive Science Society, 15* (1), 134–143.

Ohno, R. (1991). Ambient vision of the environmental perception: Describing ambient visual information. In J. Urbina-Soria, P. Ortega-Andeane, & R. Bechtel (Eds.), *Healthy environments: Proceedings of the 22nd annual conference of the Environmental Design Research Association* (pp. 237–245). Oklahoma City: Environmental Design Research Association.

Shaw, R. & Kinsella-Shaw, J. (2007). Could optical 'pushes' be inertial forces? A geometro-dynamical hypothesis. *Ecological Psychology, 19* (3), 305–320.

Stamps, A. E. & Smith, S. G. (2002). Environmental enclosure in urban areas, *Environment and Behavior, 34* (6), 781–794.

*Studies in Perception & Action X*
J. B. Wagman & C. C. Pagano (Eds.)
© 2009 Taylor & Francis Group, LLC

# Postural Response to a Suprapostural Task in Children at Risk for Developmental Coordination Disorder

Azizah Jor'dan, Michael Wade, Ken Yoshida,
& Thomas A. Stoffregen

University of Minnesota, Minneapolis, MN

Developmentally, postural stability is a critical achievement as a precursor to locomotion. Posture is not static and the exhortation to "stand still" is not possible. Standing quietly the human body oscillates at approximately 2Hz. Recording postural motion (sway) is a variable which can be investigated as a mediator of attentional effort. This study investigated how posture (a biomechanical variable that mediates coordination dynamics) is relevant to the study of movement problems in children at risk for Developmental Coordination Disorder (DCD). We proposed an experiment to determine changes in postural sway as a function of engaging in a suprapostural task requiring cognitive effort.

**Method**

Children at a local Elementary School volunteered to participate in the study. The children ranged in age from 8 yrs 9 months to 11 years ($\bar{X}$ mean age = 10 years, SD 0.72). Participants were assessed using the Movement ABC (Henderson & Sugden, 1992). Six children scored at or below the 15th percentile in the Movement ABC and were considered at risk for DCD. Five children scored well above the 15th percentile and were designated as a typically developing (TDC) control group.

Participants were asked to stand behind a designated mark 1 meter from a target. The visual task comprised two conditions; one a blank target task (BT) and the other a counting task (CT). The BT target was a plain white poster board in which participants could look anywhere within its perimeters. The CT target comprised of a stream of printed letters of the alphabet in random order. Participants were instructed to count the frequency of a designated letter during each trial. At the end of each trial, participants reported where they were in the text stream and the total number of target letters counted. We monitored movement of the head and torso.

For the CT condition, visual performance was assessed as percent accuracy (ratio of the number of letters reported to the total number present in the display). A one-sample Kolmogorov-Smirnov Test (K-S) analyzed the distribution of errors to determine any differences among the sample and the expected distribution

### Results and Discussion

*Visual performance.* The TDC and the DCD group mean percentage correct scores was 89.1% and 83.3%, respectively. The small group difference in accuracy scores may be a consequence of too low a level of task difficulty, which likely produced a ceiling effect. A more difficult or different type of task may remove the ceiling effect and increase the sensitivity to detect possible differences in postural motion between the two groups.

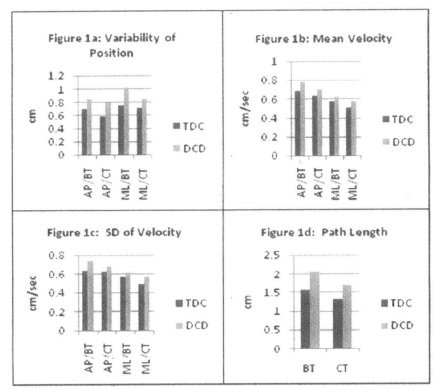

*Figure 1.* Summary of torso data. A. Variability of position. B. Mean velocity. C. Standard deviation of velocity. D. Path length. AP: Anterior-posterior. ML: Mediolateral. BT: Blank task. CT: Counting task. TDC: Typically developing children. DCD: Children at risk for developmental coordination disorder.

*Postural activity.* For movement of the head, there were no significant effects. Data for torso motion are summarized in Figure 1. We found significant main effects of Task on the mean velocity of torso motion in ML ($p$ = .027), and for the standard deviation of velocity of torso motion in the ML axis ($p$ = .012).

We sought to generate further support for the hypothesis that children at risk for DCD show different postural response characteristics when engaged in a more demanding suprapostural task. This would provided further support for data from our laboratory (Johnson & Wade, 2007); thus adding to the proposition that DCD was a perceptual motor deficit characterized by a diminished perception/action coupling when a motor response (posture) was linked to a task outcome that required increased attention and cognitive effort.

The significant task effect across groups was present for the mean velocity and the standard deviation of velocity. These findings were consistent with Stoffregen et al. (1999; 2000) in adults and Prado, Stoffregen, and Duarte (2007) in the elderly, confirming that postural stabilization of visual performance occurs at least as early as the age of children in our study. We did not find differences between the DCD and TDC groups. It may be that DCD does not alter the use of body sway in the service of visual performance. Alternatively, group differences might be obtained in new studies using a greater number of participants, and/or more demanding visual tasks.

## References

Henderson, S.E., & Sugden, D.A. (1992). Movement assessment battery for children. London: The Psychological Corporation.

Johnson, D., & Wade, M. (2007). Judgment of action capabilities in children at risk for developmental coordination disorder. *Disability and Rehabilitation, 29,* 33-45.

Prado, J., Stoffregen, T., & Duarte, M. (2007). Postural sway during dual task in young and elderly adults. *Gerontology, 53,* 274-281

Stoffregen, T. A., Pagulayan, R. J., Bardy, B. G., & Hettinger, L. J. (2000). Modulating postural control to facilitate visual performance. *Human Movement Science, 19,* 203-220.

Stoffregen, T. A., Smart, L. J., Bardy, B. G., & Pagulayan, R. J. (1999). Postural stabilization of looking. *Journal of Experimental Psychology: Human-Perception and Performance, 25,* 1641-1658.

Wade, M., Lindquist, R., Treat-Jacobson, D., & Taylor J. (1995) Optical flow, spatial orientation, and the control of posture in the elderly. *Journal of Gerontology, 50,* 51-58.

*Studies in Perception & Action X*
J. B. Wagman & C. C. Pagano (Eds.)
© 2009 Taylor & Francis Group, LLC

# Consequence of Internally Versus Externally Generated Visual Motion on Postural Regulation in a Virtual Environment: The Importance of Perception and Action Rather than Perception and Reaction

Eric Littman, Edward W. Otten & L. James Smart, Jr.

Miami University, Oxford OH

In order to achieve most goals, one must be able to successfully assess and interact with one's surroundings. These behaviors, in turn, rely on the ability to recognize the affordances that exist within a given context. Successful coordination of these activities allow for people to behave in a manner that is functional and reduces the distance between the current and goal states. These activities can be described as being future-oriented or prospective (literally, forward-looking; E.J. Gibson, 1969; Reed, 1996; Gibson & Pick, 2000) in nature. In the performance of motor tasks, the first step involves the basic control and coordination of body segments (posture; cf. Smart & Smith, 2001). When this is achieved the person is then in a position to perform subsequent actions.

In our everyday experience there exists a clear relationship between what we perceive and the actions that we produce (perception-action cycle; Gibson, 1986). This type of relation can be characterized as closed-loop in nature (where the persons actions influence and are influenced by information from the world). However, there are a number of situations where the relation between perception and action is open-looped (where the person's actions have little or no consequence on the information generated by the environment). In both cases the goal of the person is to interact successfully with the surrounding environment; it is the manner in which these interactions are accomplished that differs as a function of the type of control (internal, closed-loop or external, open-loop).

Problems can arise when an inappropriate strategy is implemented by the person; one such problem in motion venues is the occurrence of motion sickness. Through research and innovation engineers have produced better vehicles, boats, and planes that suppress the motion characteristics that make people motion sick. While the virtual reality world expands, better technology has produced more motion sickness.

Sensory conflict theory is probably the most well known and intuitive theory. The theory asserts that motion sickness is produced when the brain receives information from different senses unsynchronized with each other (reporting different motion 'realities'). While the brain attempts to resolve this conflict, one can become motion sick (Reason, 1975; Oman, 1982). Despite its intuitive appeal, Conflict Theory does not provide an objective measure of conflict, nor does it allow sickness to be predicted a priori. Postural Instability Theory, on the other hand, asserts that motion sickness is not related to a sensory conflict, but instead to a decreased ability to appropriately control one's postural motion (Riccio & Stoffregen, 1991). The longer one remains unstable, the more likely that sickness will occur. Research has shown that postural motion can predict sickness (Stoffregen & Smart, 1998; Stoffregen, et al, 2000; Smart, Stoffregen, & Bardy, 2002).

The specific goal of the study is to determine the role of control on the occurrence of motion sickness, and the ability to make prospective adjustments (actions that serve a future goal). Research has indicated that these factors can be influenced by perceived or actual control (Rolnick & Lubow, 1991). The study entailed the measurement and subsequent analysis of seated participants' postural motion while immersed in a virtual environment. It is believed that disruptions in postural control that can be produced by VEs may lead to adverse side-effects (cf. Riccio & Stoffregen, 1991) and that these effects will be more pronounced when the person is exposed to externally generated (open-loop) motion.

**Method**

Twelve undergraduate students ranging in age from 18 – 22 years. All participants had normal or corrected-to-normal vision and were in good health with no history of vestibular dysfunction or dizziness/falls. Participants received class credit for their participation. Participants were aware that there was a chance that they could become motion sick.

Motion Tracker: body movement was tracked using a magnetic tracking system (Flock of Birds, Ascension, Inc.) Four sensors were used. Motion was sampled at 40 Hz. Game console/software: A Nintendo 64 video game system, with standard controller, was used to generate the stimuli for the study. A first person shooter (Goldeneye; Rare, Inc.) was used in this study. Projector: A Sharp PG-C30XU projector was used to present the stimuli, producing an image with an unobstructed visual angle of 29° (V) x 37° (H)—distance 2.76 m.

Participants were told the nature of the study and were asked to fill out a consent form, demographics sheet, and a Simulator Sickness Questionnaire (SSQ, Kennedy, et al., 1993). Participants were asked to perform two balance checks before beginning the experiment (these were repeated before participant was allowed to leave). Participants sat on a stool, holding the game controller comfortably in their hands. Participants in each session were presented with three types of trials: 3 baseline (one post, 20 sec), 5 control (one post, 60 sec), and 6 experimental (300 sec). Three of the experimental trials used internal control (the participants were playing) and three of the trials used external control (the experimenters were playing). This is denoted by the terms active and passive, respectively.

## Results and Discussion

*Dispersional Analysis.* The basis of the dispersional analysis is to determine the spread of the probability density function at the highest level of resolution, then to lump nearest-neighbor elements of the signal together to obtain the local mean of the pair of elements. The dispersion is then calculated at this reduced level of resolution, and repeated with successively larger groupings of near neighbors. The slope of the log-log relationship between dispersion and level of resolution gives the fractal dimension D. A value of D near 1.5 is indicative of random uncorrelated noise, while a value near 1 is indicative of uniformity over all scale lengths (Bassingthwaighte, 1994).

*Anterior-Posterior*: A 2 (sick vs. well) by 2 (active vs. passive) mixed model ANOVA resulted in a significant main effect of control ($F_{(1, 12)} = 9.853$, p = .009), indicating that the value of the dispersional exponent was smaller when the participants were in control of the environment (M = 1.047, SD = .038) than when they were not in control (M = 1.096, SD = .067). There was no main effect of the condition of the participant (sick vs. well) and there was no interaction between the relative control of the participant and the condition of the participant.

Participants who became sick tended to exhibit more antipersistent (corrective) motion than participants who remained well. The results suggest that those participants who remained well were able to find an appropriate stable postural strategy while those participants who became sick were searching for such as strategy, but were not able to find one (Figure 1).

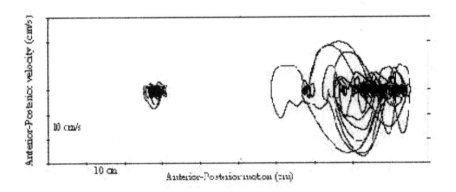

*Figure 1.* Representative Phase (AP position vs. velocity) plot for well (left) and sick (right) participants during open-loop (passive) trial.

## References

Bassingthwaighte, J. B., Liebovitch, L. S., Bruce, J. W. (1994). *Fractal Physiology.* New York, NY: Oxford University Press, Inc.

Gibson, E.J. (1969). *Principles of Perceptual Learning and Development.* East Norwalk, CT: Appleton-Century Crofts.

Gibson, J. J. (1986). *The Ecological Approach to Visual Perception.* Hillsdale, NJ: Lawrence Erlbaum Associates.

Gibson, E.J., & Pick, A.D. (2000). *An Ecological Approach to Perceptual Learning and Development.* New York: Oxford University Press.

Kennedy, R.S., Lane, N.E., Berbaum, K.S., & Lilienthal, M.G. (1993). Simulator sickness questionnaire an: enhanced method for quantifying simulator sickness. *Inter J Aviation Psychology 3*, 203—220.

Oman, C.M. (1982). A heuristic mathematical model for the dynamics of sensory conflict and motion sickness. *Acta Otolaryngol. 44 (suppl. 392)*, 1—44.

Reason, J. T., and Brand, J. J. (1975). *Motion Sickness.* London: Academic Press.

Reed, E.S. (1996). *Encountering the World: Toward an Ecological Psychology.* New York: Oxford University Press.

Riccio, G. E., & Stoffregen, T.A. (1991). An ecological theory of motion sickness and postural instability. *Ecological Psychology, 3,* 195-240.

Rolnick, A., & Lubow, R. E. (1991). Why is the driver rarely motion sick? The role of controllability in motion sickness. *Ergonomics, 34 (7),* 867 – 879.

Smart, L. J., & Smith, D. L. (2001). Postural dynamics: Clinical and empirical implications. *Journal of Manipulative and Physiological Therapeutics, 24 (5),* 340 –349.

Smart, L. J., Stoffregen, T. A., & Bardy, B. G. (2002). Visually induced motion sickness predicted by postural instability. *Human Factors, 44* (3), 451-465.

Stoffregen, T. A., Hettinger, L. R., Haas, M. W., Roe, M., & Smart, L. J. (2000). Postural instability and motion sickness in a fixed-base flight simulator. *Human Factors, 42 (3),* 458-469.

Stoffregen, T. A. & Smart, L. J. (1998). Postural instability precedes motion sickness. *Brain Research Bulletin, 47* (5), 437-448.

*Studies in Perception & Action X*
J. B. Wagman & C. C. Pagano (Eds.)
© 2009 Taylor & Francis Group, LLC

# The Effect of Open vs. Closed-Loop Optic Flow on Visually Induced Motion Sickness

Edward W. Otten & L. James Smart, Jr.

Miami University, Oxford OH

Eighteen years ago Riccio and Stoffregen (1991) asserted that motion sickness was produced by disruptions in action (postural instability) rather than deficiencies in perceptual processing (sensory conflict theory; Reason & Brand, 1975; Oman, 1990). Since then a number of studies have demonstrated that manipulating perceptual information (optic flow) can produce these behavioral disruptions and subsequent motion sickness both in natural and virtual settings (Stoffregen & Smart, 1998; Stoffregen, Hettinger, Haas, Roe, & Smart, 2000; Smart, Stoffregen, & Bardy, 2002; Smart, Otten, & Stoffregen, 2007; Villard, Flanagan, Albenese, & Stoffregen, 2008). These studies all utilized a similar mechanism as participants in all studies were exposed to motion that closely resembled that which would be produced by their own postural sway. Riccio and Stoffregen (1991) suggested that using this type of motion could be especially nauseogenic. Stoffregen and Smart (1998) attributed this potential outcome to the phenomenon of wave interference, which states that when similar waveforms come in contact with each other, the waves are disrupted; the greater the similarity between waveforms, the more catastrophic the result of the contact. We suggest that the behavioral consequence of this type of interference is that the participant will no longer be able to use the perceptual information (optic flow) obtained to effectively regulate his or her behavior.

The second similarity among these studies is that the motion produced was created artificially (computer-generated) and independent of the motion generated by the participant. While this type of stimuli in many ways represents familiar situations (movies, television, video gaming), it doesn't allow for direct testing of some of the predictions made by Riccio and Stoffregen (1991), nor does it allow for the direct testing of the importance of the nature/existence of perception-action coupling. The current study sought to address these issues by exposing participants to their own motion, in a non-coupled (playback), normal-coupled (real-time), or reverse-coupled (real-time motion phase shifted 180°) manner. It was expected that participants in the normal coupled condition would be more stable than the participants in either the reversed coupled condition or the uncoupled condition, and that sick participants would be more unstable than well participants in each condition.

## Method

Participants. Thirty participants (about 40% female with a mean age of 19.5 yrs) were recruited from the Psychology department participant pool. Ten participants were used in each condition. Thirty-seven percent (37%) reported being motion sick in the past, 46% reported no prior motion sickness, and 17% reported that they were not sure. All participants were in their normal state of health and had normal or corrected to normal vision.

Materials. One computer was used in this study to both display the stimulus through a head-mounted display (HMD; i-O Display Systems i-glasses, Menlo Park, CA), and record the motion of the participants. The HMD display had a visual angle of 18.4 degrees vertically and horizontally. The motion of the participants was captured using a magnetic tracking system (Flock of Birds; Ascension, Inc., Burlington, VT) and recorded using a software package called Vizard. The program can record motion in three axes of translation and three axes of rotation. AP head motion was used to create the movement of the stimuli. The stimulus consisted of a star field (a pattern of random white dots on a black background the translated in the anterior-posterior (AP) direction). It was displayed to simulate the "stars" at a distance of 3.3 m. The star field would change from white to red at quasi-random intervals during the experimental trials. The same software package was used to create the star field stimuli and display it to the participant.

Procedure. The participants were asked to stand comfortably in the laboratory while the researchers measured their postural sway. The experiment consisted of five 10 min trials. The first trial served to measure the baseline (without computer-generated stimulus) sway of the participant. During this trial, the participant stood in the darkened lab 3 meters from a single bright light at approximately eye height. The participant wore a set of welding goggles with the dark glass replaced with clear glass to approximate the field of view and weight of the HMD.

After the baseline trial, up to four experimental trials were conducted (depending on whether the participant became motion sick via self-report). In the **non-coupled (UC)** condition, the motion of the star field was a playback of the participant's baseline motion. In the **normal-coupled (NC)** condition, the motion was generated in real-time by the participant. In the **reverse-coupled (RC)** condition, the motion was generated in real-time by the participant, but was phase shifted 180°. In these trials the participant was exposed to the star field stimulus and asked to remember how many times the star field changed from white to red (to insure that they were paying attention to the stimulus). At the conclusion of each trial, the participant was asked 1) how many times the stimulus changed from red to white and 2) how the participant felt.

**Results and Discussion**

Motion sickness incidence: All three conditions produced motion sickness in participants, *40% in the UC* condition, *30% in the NC* condition, and *70% in the RC* condition. As in previous studies, reports of motion sickness were unambiguous and corresponded with significant increases in SSQ (Kennedy, Lane, Berbaum, & Lilienthal, 1993) scores.

Postural motion: Postural motion was analyzed using a fractal analysis called *dispersion analysis* (Bassingthwaighte, Liebovitch, & West, 1994). Like other fractal analyses (e.g., DFA; Villard, et al., 2008), this analysis measures the self-similarity of a waveform over time scale (i.e., whether smaller units of the waveform can predict the behaviour/structure of larger units of the waveform). The analysis was performed on each of the experimental trials and compared using linear contrasts (to test the specific predictions made).

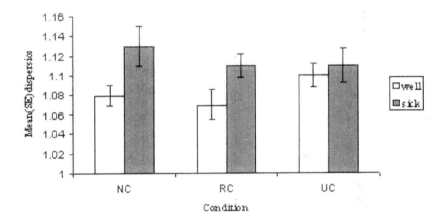

*Figure 1.* Mean (SE) dispersion values (range 1 – 1.5) as a function of condition and health, higher numbers indicate less stability (*N* =30). Note the difference between sick and well participants in the coupled conditions that is absent in the non-coupled condition.

The analysis indicated that sick participants (*M* = 1.120, *SD* = .0593) had significantly higher dispersion values than the well participants (*M* = 1.083, *SD* = .0486), *t*(86) = -2.92, *p* = .004. The analysis indicated that participants in the UC condition (*M* – 1.103, *SD* ▪ .0537) did not have significantly different dispersion values than participants in the NC and RC conditions (*M* = 1.101, *SD* = .0536), *t*(86) = .242, *p* = .809. Finally, the analysis indicated that participants in the coupled well condition (*M* = 1.079, *SD* = .0469) had significantly lower dispersion values than participants in all other conditions (*M* = 1.106, *SD* = .0552), *t*(86) = -2.253, *p* = .027 (Figure 1).

Similar to previous studies postural instability preceded reports of motion sickness. Participants who later become motion sick exhibited less fractal (self-similar) motion (indicated by higher dispersion values) than the participants who remained well, indicating a qualitative difference in the way that the groups responded to the optical motion. The fact that the sickness incidence increased dramatically when the relation between perception and action was altered suggests that the nature of the coupling matters. In particular these results suggest that the ability to anticipate, predict, and control the relation between perceptual information and action is key for maintaining stability and preventing motion sickness, and in turn lends support to concepts presented by Riccio and Stoffregen's (1991) theory.

### References

Bassingthwaighte, J. B., Liebovitch, L. S., & West, B.J. (1994). *Fractal Physiology*. New York, NY: Oxford University Press, Inc.

Kennedy, R. S., Lane, N. E., Berbaum, K. S., & Lilienthal, M. G. (1993). Simulator sickness questionnaire: An enhanced method for quantifying simulator sickness. *International Journal of Aviation Psychology, 3,* 203–220.

Oman, C. M. (1990). Motion sickness: A synthesis and evaluation of the sensory conflict theory. *Canadian Journal of Physiological Pharmacology, 68* (2), 294-303.

Reason, J.T., & Brand, J.J. (1975). *Motion sickness*. London: Academic Press.

Riccio, G. E. & Stoffregen, T. A. (1991). An ecological theory of motion sickness and postural instability. *Ecological Psychology, 3,* 195-240.

Smart, L.J., Otten, E.W. & Stoffregen, T. A. (2007). It's turtles all the way down: A comparative analysis of visually induced motion sickness. *Human Factors and Ergonomics Annual Meeting Proceedings, 51,* 1631-1634.

Smart, L.J., Stoffregen, T.A., & Bardy, B.G. (2002). Visually induced motion sickness predicted by postural instability. *Human Factors, 44*(3), 451-465.

Stoffregen, T.A., Hettinger, L.J., Haas, M.W., Roe, M.M., & Smart, L.J. (2000). Postural instability and motion sickness in a fixed-base flight simulator. *Human Factors, 42*(3), 458-469.

Stoffregen, T. A., & Smart, L.J. (1998). Postural instability precedes motion sickness. *Brain Research Bulletin, 47,* 437-448.

Villard, S.J., Flanagan, M.B., Albanese, G.M. & Stoffregen, T.A. (2008). Postural instability and motion sickness in a virtual moving room. *Human Factors, 50(2),* 332-345.

*Studies in Perception & Action X*
J. B. Wagman & C. C. Pagano (Eds.)
© 2009 Taylor & Francis Group, LLC

# Preferred Stance Width at Sea

Thomas A. Stoffregen[1], Yawen Yu[1], Fu-Chen Chen[1],
& Sebastien Villard[2]

[1]University of Minnesota, [2]University of Montpellier-1, France

Upright stance involves choices, many of which are implicit. Among these are the positioning of the feet. In side-by-side stance, we control *stance width*, that is, the distance between the feet. We also control *stance angle*, the angle between the feet. In both clinical and experimental research on stance, the values of stance width and stance angle often are not controlled, and not analyzed. In other studies, these parameters of stance are fixed by the experimenter, rather than being chosen by those standing. McIlroy and Maki (1997) took stance width and stance angle as dependent variables, asking participants to stand quietly with their feet positioned comfortably. They found that self-selected stance width tended to be approximately 17 cm.

Standing posture is of great importance at sea, and adjustments made to the control of stance are an essential part of "getting one's sea legs". Research on postural control as it relates to shipboard life has not utilized stance width or stance angle as dependent variables (e.g., Dobie et al., 2003; Nawayseh & Griffin, 2006).

We assessed self-selected stance width on two ships at sea. In one case, we first measured stance on land, and compared it to subsequent measures made at sea. In the other case, measurements taken at sea reflected changes in sea state over several days.

## Method

The study was conducted aboard the R/V Atlantis, on the 5th day of a 6-day cruise from San Diego to Mazatlan, Mexico. The Atlantis was 84 m long and displaced 3500 tons, and cruised at 12 knots. The other ship was the R/V Thomas G. Thompson, during a 10-day cruise that began in Samoa and ended in Hobart, Tasmania. The Thompson was 84 m long and displaced 3000 tons, and cruised at 11 knots. In total, 20 crewmembers (10 on each ship) participated on a volunteer basis. Crew ranged in age from 25 to 60 years, and had from 1 to 30 years experience working at sea.

Due to local conditions, procedure differed slightly on the two cruises. One day before the beginning of the Atlantis cruise, we measured the preferred stance of participants, using a nearby office provided for our use. At sea, we measured preferred stance each day for the first five days. We were not able to take terrestrial data prior to the Thompson cruise. Rather, we measured stance each of the first four days at sea, and again on the 9th day.

At sea, stance was measured separately with each participant facing forward, and facing port. In each case, the Experimenter stood approximately 3 m in front of the participant and asked him or her to take three steps forward and then stop. Using a tape measure, we measured the distance between the midline of the heels (stance width), and the distance between the great toes. The heel and toe data were used to compute stance angle.

### Results and Discussion

On the R/V Atlantis (Figure 1), sea state never exceeded 2 on the Beaufort scale (Beer, 1997). Stance width on land (19.0 cm) was similar to the report of McIlroy and Maki (1997). However, stance width at sea was greater than stance width on land, both when facing laterally (mean = 23.5 cm), $t_{(58)}$ = 2.93, $p$ = .005, and when facing forward (mean = 23.8 cm), $t_{(58)}$ = 3.14, $p$ = .003. At sea, stance width did not change over days. These effects indicate that experienced mariners selected wider stance at sea than on land, even during very mild sea states. Wider stance tends to reduce the magnitude of standing body sway (e.g., Day et al., 1993). Thus, it may be that experienced mariners use stance width as a means to modulate the magnitude of body sway. The lack of change over days (at sea) may arise from the experience of the crewmembers, from the consistent, mild sea state, or both.

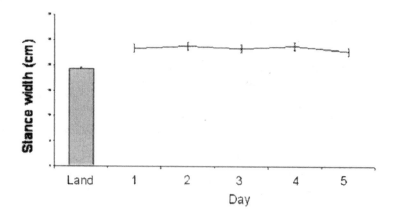

*Figure 1.* R/V Atlantis, showing stance width when facing to port.

On R/V Thomas G. Thompson, sea state varied from 3 to 4 on Days 1 – 2, from 2 to 3 on Days 3 – 4, and was at 6 on Day 9. As Figure 2 shows, stance width (when facing port) changed over days. For days 1 – 4, the slope when facing port was -0.73, which differed from 0, $p < .05$. The slope when facing forward (0.045) did not differ from 0.

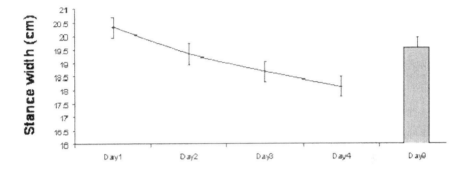

*Figure 2.* R/V Thomas G. Thompson, showing stance width when facing to port.

On R/V Thomas G. Thompson, stance width when facing port was higher than is typically observed on land (McIlroy & Maki, 1997) for the first day at sea. Over the course of the first four days at sea, stance width narrowed, and on Day 4 it was similar to what has been observed on land. The narrowing was consistent with the improving sea state over the first four days, as was the increase in stance width observed on Day 9, when the highest sea state was observed. The absence of an effect for stance when facing forward may indicate that the majority of ship motion on Thompson was in the roll plane.

We measured self-selected stance width on two ships at sea. We found differences, across the two cruises, in the effect of a ship on stance width. With consistent, mild sea states (on R/V Atlantis), stance width at sea was stable, and was wider than in the same participants on land. With variable sea states, stance width appeared to be strongly influenced by sea state. Overall, the results suggest that stance width is flexible, and that people select stance width based on local conditions. Our participants were experienced mariners. It would be interesting to see whether similar effects would obtain in persons with no previous experience at sea, and whether any adaptation in stance width would be related to possible adverse effects of sea travel, such as seasickness.

**References**

Beer, T. (1997). *Environmental oceanography.* Boca Raton, FL: CRC Press.
Dobie, T. G., May, J. G., & Flanagan, M. (2003). The influence of visual reference on stance and walking on a moving surface. *Aviation, Space, and Environmental Medicine, 74,* 838-845.

McIlroy, W. E., & Maki, B. E. (1997). Preferred placement of the feet during quiet stance: Development of a standardized foot placement for balance testing. *Clinical Biomechanics, 12,* 66-70.

Nawayseh, N., & Griffin, M. J. (2006). Effect of frequency, magnitude and direction of translational and rotational oscillation on the postural stability of standing people. *Journal of Sound and Vibration, 298,* 725–754.

*Studies in Perception & Action X*
J. B. Wagman & C. C. Pagano (Eds.)
© 2009 Taylor & Francis Group, LLC

# Infants' Visually Induced Postural Sway: The Effect of the Attractiveness of Fixation Mark

Aki Tsuruhara[1], Yasunobu Katsumata[2], Michiteru Kitazaki[2], Akitoshi Hanazawa[3], So Kanazawa[4], & Masami Yamaguchi[1,5]

[1]Chuo University, [2]Toyohashi University of Technology,
[3]Kyushu Institute of Technology, [4]Japan Women's University, [5]PRESTO, JST.

When you are on a stationary train and the train next to yours is moving, you might feel that you are moving (vection), and you might lose your balance (visually induced postural sway). It is well known that visual stimuli affect postural control and the perception of self-motion (see Howard 1982, for a review).

Visually induced sway has been regarded as the result of the misperception of self motion. More specifically, movement of large visual stimuli sometimes cause observers to perceive that they are moving and that the large visual stimuli are stationary. This misperception may cause a loss of balance.

Some previous studies, however, suggested that visually induced sway may not be due to misperception of self motion. Previc and his colleague showed that induced sway could occur before the observer perceived vection (Previc, 1992; Previc & Mullen, 1991).

Another explanation for visually induced sway is that observers try to fixate their eyes on moving stimulus, and their body sways in accordance with the moving of the stimulus (Oullier, Bardy, Stoffregen & Bootsma, 2002). Thus, the attention to the stimulus could affect visually induced sway in adults.

In this study, we examined the development of the effect of attention on visually induced sway. Developmental studies reported that visually induced postural sway has been shown in children (e.g., Lee & Aronson, 1974; Lee & Lishman, 1977) and in adults. The effect of attention on sway in infants, however, has not been clear. In our experimental trials, infants were presented with a moving background and/or a fixation mark. The attractiveness of the fixation mark was varied to control the attention of infants.

**Methods**

Participants were 7-10-month old infants (N=12). The participants were screened based on the observation and confirmation by the parents that they could sit up by themselves. Some of them could crawl, but none of them could walk by themselves.

Infants sat at the front of the 152.4cm (60 in.) screen (74.7 deg width × 59.5 deg height in visual angle), on which the stimulus display was rear-projected (Figure 1). The stimulus display was composed of a fixation mark and random-dots background. The viewing distance was maintained at approximately 80 cm.

Prior to each trial, a fixation mark turned on and off at the center of the screen, accompanied by a brief sound. When the infant looked at the fixation mark, the experimenter initiated the trial. During each trial, the fixation mark and/or random dots (background) moved leftward-rightward or just remained stationary for 2.5 s. The motion speed was modulated in raised cosine and its frequency was 0.2Hz, so that the movement started at the center of the screen and went leftward or rightward and then came back in the opposite movement. The maximum speed of the motion was 11.9 deg/s or 19.3 deg/s, but the results did not differ significantly, so we combined them in analysis.

The attractiveness of the fixation mark (attractive character / simple square), the movement of the background (motion / no motion), and the movement of the fixation mark (motion / no motion) were varied, and all combinations were presented to each infant. The behavior of the infant was videotaped throughout the experiment. Only the infant's looking behavior was visible in the video. One observer (rater), who was unaware of the stimulus identity, judged whether the infants looked at the screen, and whether the infants' gaze and posture changed on each trial. Additionally, the movements of the infants were quantified and judged by analyzing the video-image sequences through a computer image analysis detecting the movement of body parts.

*Figure 1*. The experimental setting.

## Results and Discussion

The ratios of the gaze and the postural movements were calculated for each infant in each condition by dividing the number of the trials in which the gaze or posture of the infant moved by the total number of the trials in which the infant looked at the screen. The mean ratio of the gaze and the postural movement are shown in Figure 2 and Figure 3, respectively.

The ratio of the gaze movements seemed to differ between the attractive and non-attractive fixation mark conditions. When only the fixation mark moved, infants moved their gaze more in the attractive fixation mark condition than in the non-attractive fixation mark condition. This result indicates that the attractive fixation mark was actually attractive to the infants in this study.

The ratio of the postural movements showed that infants moved their body with the stimulus to which infants did not pay attention. In general, postural movements were in response to the movement of background rather than movement of a fixated stimulus. On the moving background, postural sway increased with the movement of the attractive fixation mark than the movement of the non-attractive fixation mark. These results differ from results with adults showing postural movements in response to the movement of fixated stimulus.

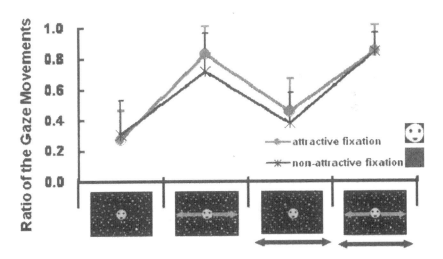

*Figure 2.* Mean ratios of the gaze movements. Error bars indicates standard deviations.

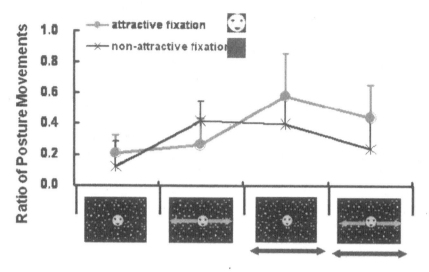

*Figure 3.* Mean ratios of the posture movements. Error bars indicates standard deviations.

### References

I. P. Howard. Human visual orientation. New York: John Wiley & Sons. 1982.

D. N. Lee & E. Aronson. Visual proprioceptive control of standing in human infants. *Perception and Psychophysics*, **15**, 529-532, 1974.

D. N. Lee & J. R. Lishman: Visual proprioceptive control of stance. *Journal of Human Movement Studies*, **1**, 87-95, 1975.

O. Oullier, B. G. Bardy, T. A. Stoffregen & R. J. Bootsma. Postural coordination in looking and tracking tasks. *Human Movement Science,* **21,** 147-167, 2002.

F. H. Previc & M. Donnelly. The effects of visual depth and eccentricity on manual bias, induced motion, and vection. *Perception*, **22**, 929-945, 1993.

F. H. Previc & T. J. Mullen. A comparison of the latencies of visually induced postural change and self-motion perception. *Journal of Vestibular Research*, **1**, 317-23, 1991.

*Acknowledgements.* This study was supported by PRESTO, JST and a Grant-in-Aid for scientific research (18300090, 20539004) from JSPS.

*Studies in Perception & Action X*
J. B. Wagman & C. C. Pagano (Eds.)
© 2009 Taylor & Francis Group, LLC

# Body Sway in the Processes of Perceiving Various Visual Environmental Structures

Chih-Mei (Melvin) Yang & Chia-Chun Huang

Department of Physical Education, National Taiwan Normal University, Taipei, Taiwan

The coupling between perception and action allows for successful behavior in an environment. Affordances are opportunities for behavior that reflect the relationship between action-relevant properties of the environment and the action producing capabilities of an individual (Gibson, 1979; Stoffregen, 2003; cf. Turvey, 1992). Furthermore, from the perspective of ecological psychology, animals act to perceive and perceive to act, so they can promote their perception of affordances by way of action. Optic flow elicited by the movements of the individual or environment moving objects can provide the specific information of the environment (Gibson, 1979), and individuals can use it to perceive affordances.

It is impossible to stand without some degree of body sway. Traditionally, body sway was regarded noise while keeping balance. However, Riccio and Stoffregen (1991) thought that body sway might provide functions other than just maintaining balance. They pointed out that the body sway can facilitate perception of the suprapostural information.

This study was conducted to investigate the change in body sway in the processes of perceiving various visual environment structures. The research question was: Is the different body sway generated when individuals perceive different environmental structures?

Based on the theoretic frame of the perception-and-action coupling, we hypothesized that in different environmental conditions, individuals would employ different body sway for using optic flow to perceive more information.

## Method

There were 12 young adults (age 20-40) who participated in this experiment. They were healthy, had normal vision, and reported no vestibule or balance-related disease. A Polhemus LIBERTY system and a MotionMonitor motion capture system were used for collecting body sway data. The experimental set-up included five different colors of surround curtains (black, white, gross mosaic, and fine mosaic, see Figure 1).

*Figure 1.* Experimental set-up.

The participants were required to stand naturally for 40 seconds in 6 conditions: 1) close eyes; and open eyes facing the following environmental structure: 2) normal room structure; 3) all-white curtain; 4) all-black curtain; 5) fine mosaic curtain; and 6) gross mosaic curtain. Participants completed all conditions standing on the ground. In addition, they completed conditions 2 through 5 while standing on an 8 cm wide by 40 cm long bar set in both a medial-lateral and anterior-posterior orientation (see Figure 1).

There were 7200 points of body positions recorded at 240 Hz during the middle 30 seconds in each trial. Standard deviations (SDs) for each trial were calculated for body sway, and then were statistically analyzed by one-way repeated design ANOVAs in standing conditions and sway directions separately.

**Results and Discussion**

1. Standing on the ground

Body sway did not differ in the five experimental surroundings ($F(4, 55)$ = 0.315, $p$ = .580, $\eta^2$=.014)). This result shows that the body sway of participants was not influenced by the change in surroundings and the hypothesis was not supported. But another possibility for this finding is that this it is quite easy to induce body sway in this condition. See Figure 2.

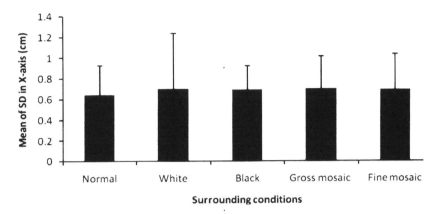

*Figure 2.* Body sway in standing on the ground condition.

## 2. Standing on the anterior-posterior set wooden bar

There were differences in body sway while standing on the barest in the anterior-posterior direction. Such differences shows that the body sway is significantly more stable while facing the gross mosaic surrounding ($F(4, 55) = 4.786$, $p < .05$, $\eta^2 = .232$). This result means the different surroundings do induce the counterparts in sway. See Figure 3.

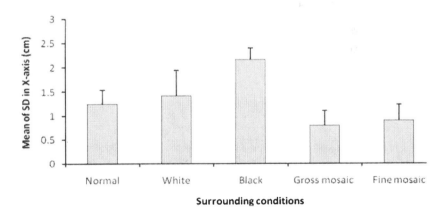

*Figure 3.* Body sway in standing on the anterior-posterior set wooden bar.

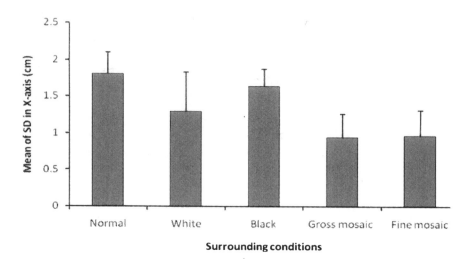

*Figure 4.* Body sway in standing on the mediolateral set wooden bar.

### 3. Standing on the mediolateral set wooden bar

This result is similar to the last condition. It shows that there is significantly different body sway while facing different structures of surroundings ($F(4, 55) = 4.630, p < .05, \eta^2 = .214$). See Figure 4.

Based on the data from the experimental manipulations, we concluded that individuals exert different body sway to perceive the information of the environment for maintaining balance when the balance task is sufficiently difficult

### References

Gibson, J. J. (1979). *The ecological approach to visual perception.* Hillsdale, NJ: Lawrence Erlbaum.

Riccio, G. E., & Stoffregen, T. A. (1991). An ecological theory of motion sickness and postural instability. *Ecological Psychology, 3,* 195-240.

Stoffregen, T. A. (2003). Affordance as properties of the animal-environment system. *Ecological Psychology, 15,* 115-134.

Turvey, M. T. (1992). Affordances and prospective control: An outline of the ontology. *Ecological Psychology, 4,* 173-187.

*Studies in Perception & Action X*
J. B. Wagman & C. C. Pagano (Eds.)
© 2009 Taylor & Francis Group, LLC

# Body Sway and Visual Performance at Sea

Yawen Yu[1], Yasunobu Katsumata[2], & Thomas A. Stoffregen[1]

[1]University of Minnesota, [2]Toyohashi University of Technology, Japan

Postural control actions serve to maintain the body's center of mass above the base of support, which prevents falling. Body sway moves the center of mass but it also moves the head and, thereby, influences the position and motion of the eyes. For this reason, sway can either inhibit or support stabilization of the eyes relative to the illuminated environment. We have shown that the magnitude of body sway is reduced during performance of demanding visual tasks, such as reading (Stoffregen et al., 2000), and that such reductions are related to ocular stabilization, rather than to cognitive components of tasks (Stoffregen et al., 2007). In the present study, we examined postural stabilization of vision in a situation involving motion of the surface of support.

We stand and walk by pushing against the support surface. The kinematic consequences of a given muscle contraction are influenced by the dynamics of the support surface, such as its length, rigidity, and friction (Riccio & Stoffregen, 1988). A special type of support surface dynamics occurs when the support surface is moving, as happens in vehicles (Stoffregen & Riccio, 1988). A classic instance of this case is life at sea. "Getting your sea legs" is one of the oldest types of perceptual-motor adaptation known to humanity. Impelled by wind and waves, ships are in continuous oscillatory motion. Unlike an icy sidewalk, we cannot escape from the challenging dynamics of a ship; we must cope with the ship's motion continuously. For this reason, ships make an ideal laboratory for the study of long-term perceptual-motor adaptation.

We studied experienced maritime crewmembers on a ship at sea. Relations between body motion and the performance of visual tasks are of increasing importance in naval applications, as work becomes increasingly focused on computer interaction. While at sea, standing participants performed difficult and easy visual vigilance tasks. We predicted that sway would be reduced during performance of the difficult task, relative to stance during performance of the easy task (cf. Stoffregen et al., 2007). We also varied stance width, that is, the distance between the feet during stance. Wider stance is associated with reductions in the magnitude of spontaneous postural sway (e.g., Day et al., 1993). We predicted that the magnitude of sway would be negatively related to stance width.

## Method

The study was conducted aboard the R/V Thomas G. Thompson, during a 10-day cruise that began in Samoa and ended in Hobart, Tasmania. The Thompson was 84 m long and displaced 3000 tons, and cruised at 11 knots. Ten crewmembers participated on a volunteer basis. Crew ranged in age from 26 to 60 years, and had from 5 to 30 years experience working at sea.

Postural data were collected using a force plate (AMTI). Visual stimuli were generated using custom software on a PC laptop, and were presented on a 19-inch flat screen video monitor. The video monitor was affixed to a cabinet so that its center was 1.7 m above the floor.

Participants stood on the force plate with their heels on a line that was 1.0 m from the screen. Lateral foot placement was determined by three pairs of lines on the plate, such that the heels were 5 cm, 17 cm or 30 cm apart. Participants performed visual vigilance tasks. Visual targets consisted of pairs of lines that appeared on the screen, against a white background. In each pair, the lines either were the same length (distracters) or were of different lengths (critical signals). Targets appeared for 200 ms, and there was one target per second. For the Easy task, the lines were solid black. For the Hard task, the lines were pale gray. The hard task was equivalent to the one used by Stoffregen et al. (2007). The sequencing of distracters and critical signals was randomized. There were 20 critical signals per trial. Each trial was 60 s long. Participants held a wireless mouse. They were instructed to ignore distracters, and to push the left button on the mouse for each critical signal. The laptop recorded the button presses. On each day, we used a $2 \times 3$ design with one trial per participant in each of six conditions. Each trial was 60 s long. Participants were tested each day for 4 days. Easy and Hard trials were blocked, and stance widths were randomized within blocks. During testing, sea state varied from 3 to 4 (on the Beaufort scale; Beer, 1997) on Days $1 - 2$, from 2 to 3 on Days $3 - 4$.

We evaluated visual task performance using signal detection theory. The rates of hits (correct button presses) and false alarms (incorrect button presses) were combined to yield d', a widely used measure of vigilance performance (Craig, 1984). We assessed postural activity in terms of the positional variability of the COP in the AP and ML axes.

## Results and Discussion

The overall mean for d' was 4.28 for the Easy task, and 3.55 for the Hard task. These means differed, $F_{(1,6)} = 16.16$, $p = .007$, confirming that the Easy task was less difficult than the Hard task.

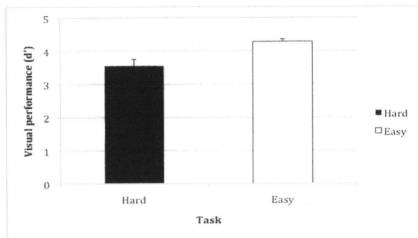

*Figure 1.* Visual performance (d'), showing the effect of visual task.

For postural sway, the results are summarized in Figure 2. For movement in the body's AP axis, analysis of variance revealed a significant main effect of task, $F_{(1,9)} = 5.37$, $p = .046$, and a significant main effect of day, $F_{(3,7)} = 17.91$, $p = .001$. The main effect of stance width was not significant, and there were no significant effects in the ML axis. The main effect of task confirmed our prediction, and replicates our land-based studies relating postural control to visual performance. The absence of a main effect of stance width on sway suggests that wider stance may not be used to minimize sway at sea.

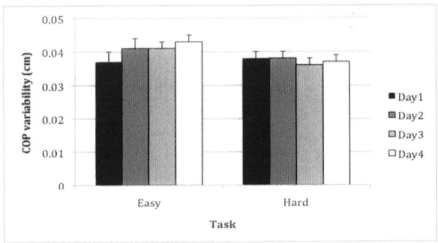

*Figure 2.* Positional variability of the COP in the body's AP axis for the Easy and Hard tasks, as a function of days.

Historically, work at sea has consisted primarily of physical labor. Increasingly, however, physical labor is being replaced by human-computer interaction, much of which consists of the monitoring of computer displays. Thus, our visual vigilance tasks are relevant to significant components of contemporary work at sea. Our results demonstrate that postural control actions can be tuned in ways that tend to support visual performance and that such tuning exists in crewmembers who are fully acclimated to shipboard conditions. Ships offer a natural laboratory for the study of perceptual-motor adaptation under dynamic conditions. Research of this kind can have direct relevance to issues of crew performance, but also to basic theories of perceptual-motor control and learning.

## References

Beer, T. (1997). *Environmental oceanography*. Boca Raton, FL: CRC Press.

Craig, A. (1984). Human engineering: The control of vigilance. In J. S. Warm (Ed.), *Sustained attention in human performance* (pp. 247-282). New York: Wiley.

Day, B.L., Steiger, M.J., Thompson, P.D., & Marsen, C.D. (1993). Effects of vision and stance width on human body motion when standing: implications for afferent control of lateral sway. *Journal of Physiology, 469*, 479-499.

Riccio, G. E., & Stoffregen, T. A. (1988). Affordances as constraints on the control of stance. *Human Movement Science, 7,* 265-300.

Stoffregen, T. A., Hove, P., Bardy, B. G.; Riley, M., & Bonnet, C. T. (2007). Postural stabilization of perceptual but not cognitive performance. *Journal of Motor Behavior, 39*, 126-138.

Stoffregen, T. A., Pagulayan, R. J., Bardy, B. G., & Hettinger, L. J. (2000). Modulating postural control to facilitate visual performance. *Human Movement Science, 19*, 203-220.

Stoffregen, T. A., & Riccio, G. E. (1988). An ecological theory of orientation and the vestibular system. *Psychological Review, 95,* 3-14.

*Acknowledgements.* We thank Captain Alan McClenaghan and Daniel Schwartz, University of Washington School of Oceanography, who made this study possible.

*Studies in Perception & Action X*
J. B. Wagman & C. C. Pagano (Eds.)
© 2009 Taylor & Francis Group, LLC

# Author Index

# Keyword Index